T0037293

The Little Book of

NORTH
AMERICAN
MAMMALS

BUSHEL & PECK BOOKS

Text copyright © 2022 by Robert Miles

Published by Bushel & Peck Books, www.bushelandpeckbooks.com.
All rights reserved. No part of this publication may be reproduced without written
permission from the publisher.

Bushel & Peck Books is dedicated to fighting illiteracy all over the world.
For every book we sell, we donate one to a child in need——book for book.
To nominate a school or organization to receive free books,
please visit www.bushelandpeckbooks.com.

Type set in Temeraire, Avenir Next, and Bebas.

Illustrations sourced from the Biodiversity Heritage Library. Other image credits as follows:
vine pattern: Nespola Designs/Shutterstock.com; graph paper background: Vector Image
Plus/Shutterstock.com. Animal taxonomy sourced from Wikipedia.

ISBN: 9781638190059

First Edition

Printed in the United States

10 9 8 7 6 5 4 3 2 1

The Little Book of
NORTH AMERICAN MAMMALS

ROBERT MILES

CONTENTS

GOT MILK?

If someone says "cow," the first word that pops into your head will probably be "milk." Yet there are other kinds of milk: wolf milk, elk milk, even rabbit milk. In fact, lots of animals make milk, because milk is the defining feature of all mammals.

Domestic
Cattle

1. CATTLE

Cattle are the headline species of the family *Bovidae*. They're large, grazing animals that have been domesticated for thousands of years. Most are kept as livestock, though some are feral (domesticated animals that return to the wild). Cattle are used as beasts of burden and raised for their hides, milk, and meat, which is known as beef. The most famous breed of cattle, the Texas Longhorn, played a major role in establishing the cowboy culture of the American West—roundups, cattle drives, chuckwagons, stampedes, the works. Looking at a cow's face with its blank, bovine stare, it's easy to think that these are unintelligent animals. Yet some research suggests that cows can recognize other cows and even some people, too. They can learn and remember, have emotions like fear and anxiety, and even have individual personalities. Hmm, food for thought.

CLASSIFICATION

KINGDOM: *Animalia*

PHYLUM: *Chordata*

CLASS: *Mammalia*

ORDER: *Artiodactyla*

FAMILY: *Bovidae*

SUBFAMILY: *Bovinae*

GENUS: *Bos*
(Wild and domestic cattle)

BY THE NUMBERS

10,500 YEARS	*The number of years humans have domesticated cattle.*
80	*The number of breeds of cattle in the United States alone.*
6 GALLONS	*The amount of milk a Holstein Friesian cow produces each day.*

LARGER THAN LIFE

The first thing you notice when coming face to face with a bison bull is the sheer size of the beast. It's as if a mountain suddenly sprouted legs and began walking. Bison are the largest land mammals in North America and can weigh over a ton. They're all muscle, too, with huge "upper" bodies and narrow waists. They look like bovine weightlifters! Yet for such bulky beasts, they are remarkably quick and agile, capable of sprinting forty miles per hour and jumping eight feet from a standing start. In the old days, just imagine how the ground would shake, rock, and roll as hundreds of thousands of these beasts thundered over the earth.

American Bison

2. BISON

Bison are related to cattle and once roamed over nearly all of North America, with most dwelling in the great central plains. There is no more iconic American animal, with its great shaggy head, huge hump, scraggly beard, and short, curved horns. For this reason, the American Bison was recently designated the American National Mammal. Though bison are commonly called "buffalo," biologists insist that true buffalo (like the water buffalo) are found only in Africa and Asia and that America's buffalo is, in fact, a bison. Whatever you call them, they're considered sacred to plains Indian tribes like the Sioux and Cheyenne and were once at the very heart of their economy and culture. But they were hunted relentlessly by European colonists until only a few hundred remained (the most dramatic species decline ever recorded). Fortunately, that number has recovered significantly, but it's still a fraction of what used to exist.

CLASSIFICATION

KINGDOM: *Animalia*

PHYLUM: *Chordata*

CLASS: *Mammalia*

ORDER: *Artiodactyla*

FAMILY: *Bovidae*

SUBFAMILY: *Bovinae*

SUBTRIBE: *Bovina*

GENUS: *Bison (Bison)*

BY THE NUMBERS

40-60 MILLION	*The number of bison that once roamed over North America*
400,000	*The estimated number of bison living today.*
6 FEET	*Average height of a bison (at the shoulder ridge).*

DIRT BAGS

Bison love to flop on the ground and roll in dirt. It's called wallowing. In places where bison wallow repeatedly, the ground gets hollowed out like a bowl. These are called buffalo wallows. Bison roll in dirt to get relief from biting insects.

Males of many species, especially those in the Bovidae *and* Cervidae *families, participate in something called the rut. During the annual rut, all mature males must battle (usually violently) for the right to mate with females.*

Bighorn
Sheep

3. WILD SHEEP

There are two kinds of wild sheep in North America: Bighorn sheep (*Ovis canadensis*) and Dall sheep (*Ovis dali*). Bighorns, as the name suggests, have really big horns that loop in spectacular spirals on either side of their heads. Though females (ewes) have horns too, they're little things and only slightly curved. It's the rams (males) that have the famous big horns. Dall Sheep are adapted to life in the far north and are similar to Bighorns, only they're white and have thinner horns. The hooves of both species are specially designed for rock climbing. The outside is hard, but the inside is spongy. This spongy core molds to uneven rock surfaces, providing excellent grip and traction, while the hard outer edge bites into rock and holds fast. This adaptation allows wild sheep to scale impressive cliffs, which is an excellent way to escape predators. Nyah, nyah, can't catch me.

CLASSIFICATION

KINGDOM: *Animalia*

PHYLUM: *Chordata*

CLASS: *Mammalia*

ORDER: *Artiodactyla*

FAMILY: *Bovidae*

SUBFAMILY: *Caprinae*

TRIBE: *Caprini*

GENUS: *Ovis*
(Wild and domestic sheep)

BY THE NUMBERS

30 POUNDS	The average weight of a Bighorn ram's horns.
2 INCHES	The minimum cliff-ledge width that a Bighorn can stand on, thanks to their excellent balance.
8 TIMES	The force of Bighorn smashups can be eight times greater than the force necessary to smash a human skull.

Dall Sheep

WHY THEY'RE CALLED RAMS

The climax of the bighorn rut is rammin' time. Rams rear up on their hind legs and launch themselves at each other, bashing heads with tremendous force. Fortunately, they have an extra layer of bone in their skulls that makes them quite hard headed.

OH SWEAT, ELIXIR OF LIFE!

Like all mammals, goats need salt (sodium) to survive. However, there isn't much sodium in plants, so plant eaters, like goats, must find other sources of salt. Normally, they get it by licking certain rocks that contain salts and other minerals. These are called salt licks. But mountain goats have discovered another way to satisfy their salt cravings: human pee. That's right, your pee has lots of salt. So does your sweat. And in national parks, there are hordes of sweaty people peeing everywhere. So, goats have begun lingering near trails and campsites, attracted by the people's pee and sweat. They ransack tents looking for sweaty clothes and lick bushes hikers have used as Porta-Potties.

Rocky
Mountain
Goat

4. MOUNTAIN GOAT

The mountain goat (*Oreamnos americanus*) is called a goat, but it's more closely related to antelopes. It has all-white fur, a prominent beard, and bushy legs that look like baggy pants. It's probably the least-studied large mammal in North America, partly because it's so hard to get to! True to their name, mountain goats are usually found in steep, rugged mountains, often above 13,000 feet. They're true skyscrapers! Staying close to rocky cliffs is important to them—that's their best escape route from predators. The mountain goat is probably the world's top mountaineer, better even than Bighorn sheep. They have strong legs and powerful shoulder muscles that make climbing cliffs a breeze. Getting a grip is easy for them, too, thanks to special rock-gripping hooves, similar in design to those of Bighorn. Up, up, and away!

KINGDOM: *Animalia*

PHYLUM: *Chordata*

CLASS: *Mammalia*

ORDER: *Artiodactyla*

FAMILY: *Bovidae*

SUBFAMILY: *Caprinae*

TRIBE: *Caprini*

GENUS: *Oreamnos*

SPECIES: *O. americanus (Mountain goat)*

BY THE NUMBERS

12 FEET	*Distance a mountain goat can jump from standing start.*
3-4	*The number of conflicts a typical mountain goat gets into each* **hour**.
12 INCHES	*Maximum length of horns on a male. Female horns can reach nine inches.*

CLIFFHANGERS

Though they might actually poke each other with their horns when riled, mountain goats usually prefer head butting, horn waving, and pushing and shoving. Of course, pushing and shoving is not a good idea on a cliff when you're literally living on the edge. Good as they are up high, goats can fall when pushed (but not as often as you might think).

13

White-Tailed Deer (Male)

White-Tailed Deer (Female)

ONE WAY TO AVOID POOPY DIAPERS

Does (female deer) can have one to three babies, called fawns. Since many animals love to eat fawns, they have to be good at hiding to survive. Not having any scent glands yet, fawns have no smell that might attract predators. Also, the mother deer licks each fawn obsessively after touching it to remove her own scent. Each day when the mother is away feeding, the fawns must lay motionless until she returns. If one needs to go potty, it will just have to wait. When the mother comes home, she leads her near-bursting babies to a safe spot where they can relieve themselves. Then, she eats the poop or laps up the pee to remove her babies' scent. The things moms do for their kids!

5. DEER

Deer are herbivores, or plant eaters. They're also "cud" chewers, or ruminants. Surviving on a steady diet of plants is no easy trick, and deer couldn't do it with a stomach like yours or mine. They require a larger, four-chambered design capable of digesting tough plant fibers. When eating, a deer typically gulps her food, chewing it just enough to slip it down into her stomach's first chamber. Later, in a safe spot, she regurgitates the half-chewed plants into her mouth. This is the cud. Then she sits there with half-closed eyes, happily chewing her cud for a spell. This is called ruminating. When thoroughly pulverized, the cud is re-swallowed. Now it enters the second stomach chamber, where microorganisms digest the tough plant fibers. Finally, it passes into the last two chambers where further digestion and absorption of nutrients takes place.

CLASSIFICATION

KINGDOM: *Animalia*

PHYLUM: *Chordata*

CLASS: *Mammalia*

ORDER: *Artiodactyla*

FAMILY: *Cervidae*

SUBFAMILY: *Capreolinae (New World deer)*

BY THE NUMBERS

30 MILLION	*The estimated deer population today, most of which are white-tailed deer and mule deer.*
7-10 DAYS AFTER BIRTH	*Time it takes before fawns are strong enough to follow their mother on feeding trips.*
30 MILES PER HOUR	*Maximum sprinting speed of deer.*

BONEHEADS

Deer, like all members of the deer family Cervidae, *grow antlers, in contrast to animals in the* Bovidae *family, like cattle, which grow horns. Both antlers and horns are made of bone, so what's the difference? Antlers are typically grown only by males and are branched or forked. Horns are grown by both sexes and are unbranched.*

Eastern
Woodland
Caribou

6. CARIBOU

Caribou are the deer family's cold-weather specialists. You're probably more familiar with the name they go by in Europe: reindeer. Caribou and reindeer are actually both subspecies of the species *Rangifer tarandus*. They live in the far North and love to live in herds. Usually, there are just 10 to 100 of them, but when traveling they can form super-herds of 50,000 to 500,000 animals—that's a lot of Rudolphs! Caribou must travel to find food, and since food is scarce in the far north, they might need to journey 3,000 miles each year. Reindeer were domesticated many years ago and are still raised for their milk, meat, hides, and antlers. People also use them as draft animals to pull sleds. The meat is actually quite tasty and nutritious, and in Norway, you can find smoked reindeer, grilled reindeer, and even reindeer pizza.

CLASSIFICATION

KINGDOM: *Animalia*

PHYLUM: *Chordata*

CLASS: *Mammalia*

ORDER: *Artiodactyla*

FAMILY: *Cervidae*

SUBFAMILY: *Capreolinae*

TRIBE: *Rangiferini*

GENUS: *Rangifer*

SPECIES: *R. tarandus*
(*Caribou/reindeer*)

BY THE NUMBERS

25% — Reindeer noses have 25% more tiny blood vessels than human noses have. This warms the frosty air as it's breathed in and makes all reindeer "red-nosed reindeer."

4 YEARS — The average lifespan of a male is four years less than that of a female

50 MILES PER HOUR — Maximum speed of a reindeer—they're fast.

LOVE HURTS

Caribou bucks must do battle in the rut arena like every other male in the deer family. Yet win or lose, rutting takes a toll on each and every warrior. They must enter winter, the most difficult time of the year to find food, already half-starved. Bucks can also emerge from the arena so battered and torn that they fall easy prey to wolves or bears.

BOOGIE WOOGIE BUGLE BOYS

Elk bulls roar their hearts out during rutting season—in fact, "rut" comes from the Latin word for "roar." Yet the elk "roar" is not like a lion's roar. It's more often referred to as a "bugle." What an elk bugle actually sounds like depends on who's listening. If you're a person, it's just about the most hideous sound ever, like fingernails scraping over a chalkboard attached to an amplifier cranked at full volume. But if you're an elk lady, the bugle is an irresistibly beautiful love song. On the other hand, if you're an elk bull, it's a call to battle. Charge!

American Elk

7. ELK (WAPITI)

Elk (*Cervus canadensis*) are large members of the deer family and are found mainly in western North America and central Asia. They look like regular deer, only bigger, with distinct white rump patches. They're sometimes called wapiti, which comes from the Shawnee word for "white." White-butts (wapiti) mate in the fall. At this time, the males must compete for females in the annual rut, just like those in many other species. Then, the elk babies arrive in May or June and are called calves, not fawns. Being highly social animals, elk form large, single-sex herds. They spend the winter at lower elevations, then migrate to higher-elevations in summer. They were once over hunted, and even today, they are a popular big-game animal.

CLASSIFICATION

KINGDOM: *Animalia*

PHYLUM: *Chordata*

CLASS: *Mammalia*

ORDER: *Artiodactyla*

FAMILY: *Cervidae*

SUBFAMILY: *Cervinae*

GENUS: *Cervus*

SPECIES: *C. canadensis (Elk/wapiti)*

BY THE NUMBERS

20%	The percentage of body weight usually lost by bull elk during the rut.
1,200 POUNDS	Weight of a large bull of the Roosevelt elk subspecies.
8 FEET	Height of obstacles that elk can jump over. Wow!

ROMANCE, ELK STYLE

How can a bull elk make himself attractive to the elk ladies? Well, rubbing his antlers against trees and bushes helps. So does digging up the earth. Wallowing in mud mixed with his urine is good, too. Of course, this may seem disgusting to us, but what do we know?

19

Moose
(Male)

RACKING HIS BRAINS

Moose start sprouting antlers when just a year old, and they get bigger and more elaborate each year. They can reach truly awesome sizes. Antlers are used mainly during the annual rut. After that, a bull has no need for such heavy, cumbersome headgear, so the antlers just drop off, plop! This helps conserve energy during the lean winter months. Yet when spring arrives, each bull must grow a whole new set, starting from scratch.

8. MOOSE

Perhaps no North American animal is quite as impressive up close as a fully-antlered bull moose. Moose (*Alces alces*) are the largest members of the deer family and are often six to seven feet tall at the shoulders. Including the head and antlers, they can tower ten feet high, stretch eight to ten feet in length, and weigh up to 1,800 pounds—in other words, they're huge! With a long, homely face and a droopy upper lip, a moose's face looks rather like a horse's (they're not related). Since they have such long, lanky legs, moose appear to be walking on stilts, giving them a clumsy appearance. But don't be fooled— they can run up to thirty-five miles per hour and can easily run you down. These animals don't mind the cold, even extreme cold, though they do get hot and bothered by warm temperatures. Since moose easily overheat, their range is limited to colder, more northerly places.

BY THE NUMBERS

1 INCH PER DAY	*How fast bull moose antlers can grow.*
70 POUNDS	*The amount of food moose can consume each day during the plentiful summer months.*
6 FEET	*The spread (or width) of a large set of moose antlers.*

ROCKY-MOUNTAIN CAR WASH

Being herbivores, moose need sources of salt (sodium). Many tons of salt get dumped on our roadways each winter to melt ice, and this gets smeared all over our cars. When people in moose country pull over to the side of the road to observe passing moose, sometimes the animals come up to the vehicles to lick off the salt.

21

PIG HEADED

Pigs are complex creatures. They show a wide range of emotions, love to play, and have individual personalities. Pigs are one of the most intelligent animals on the planet—smarter even than dogs. They're remarkably fast learners with excellent memories. Also, pigs seem to have a strong sense of self; a porker can recognize its own face in a mirror, something only a few animals can do. Pigs can even play video games. Porknite, anyone?

DON'T SWEAT IT

Nobody "sweats like a pig," not even pigs. That's because pigs don't sweat. They hardly have any sweat glands! Since they can't cool off by sweating, they roll in mud. It also helps them get rid of parasites, like ticks.

Domestic
Pig
(Female)

9. PIGS

All pigs are descendants of the Eurasian wild boar. Pigs are true omnivores. They can eat almost anything—and usually do. In olden times, people noticed pigs eating garbage, feces (poop), and even the bodies of executed criminals. This grossed them out so much that they wouldn't eat pork anymore. Many people still won't. Pigs are very good at digging for food with their tough snouts. This is called rooting. In frontier days, all a farmer had to do was let his pigs wander in the woods, and they would feed themselves. Then whenever he wanted pork, he could just go out and collect one of his hogs. This was called free-range hog raising.

CLASSIFICATION

KINGDOM: *Animalia*

PHYLUM: *Chordata*

CLASS: *Mammalia*

ORDER: *Artiodactyla*

FAMILY: *Suidae*

GENUS: *Sus*

SPECIES: *S. domesticus*
(Domestic pig)

BY THE NUMBERS

2,000	*Pigs can smell 2,000 times better than you can, though their eyesight isn't so great.*
1 MILLION	*Estimated number of pigs kept as pets in the U.S. and Canada.*
2	*Number of litters a sow can have every twelve to fifteen months, starting out with four to six piglets when young and increasing with age to ten to thirteen.*

MR. CLEAN

Most people think pigs are filthy animals, yet pigs are actually quite clean. If given a choice, they won't poop or pee where they eat or sleep. Unfortunately, they're rarely given the choice. In fact, much of the filth associated with pigs can be blamed on how they're raised. You try staying clean in a cramped, overcrowded pigsty.

23

GOING HOG WILD

When pigs go wild, they really go wild. Over time, they revert back to their wild roots. They get hairier, grow tusks, and become more aggressive. Then the destruction begins. They damage crops and property. They muscle out native species—or simply eat them. Worst of all, they're super hard to control because they breed so fast and are so smart.

Wild Boar

10. WILD PIGS

In addition to farm pigs, we also have plenty of wild pigs in North America. Ever since Hernando de Soto brought the first ones to the mainland in 1539, pigs have been escaping and scampering back into the wild. People would even release them on purpose. This might be because they were practicing free-range hog raising, or maybe because they wanted animals to hunt. During the late 1800s, wealthy hunters also imported and released Eurasian wild boar here. So, today's wild hogs are a motley mix of all of these, and this mixed ancestry is the source of their power. Genetic diversity gives them toughness and resistance to disease. Their inner wild-boar makes them hardy and aggressive. Their barnyard ancestry gives them the ability to produce large litters and grow to massive sizes. And of course they're crazy smart. Many scientists now think wild hogs are a kind of super pig.

CLASSIFICATION

KINGDOM: *Animalia*

PHYLUM: *Chordata*

CLASS: *Mammalia*

ORDER: *Artiodactyla*

FAMILY: *Suidae*

GENUS: *Sus*

SPECIES: *S. scrofa (Feral pig)*

BY THE NUMBERS

30 MILES PER HOUR	*Sprinting speed of a typical wild pig—about twice as fast as a domestic pig.*
$2 BILLION	*Estimated cost of all the damage caused by wild pigs in the U.S.*
9 MILLION	*The number of feral pigs believed to be living wild in the U.S.—that's 9 million and rising!*

NEED YOUR FIELD PLOWED, MISTER?

Wild hogs travel in sounders. This is a group of two or more mature sows (females) and their youngsters, sometimes thirty to forty in all. When these hog gangs are on the prowl at night, nothing is safe. A field of carefully-tended crops at sundown will look like a bomb-cratered no man's land by dawn.

Collared Peccary

VIVA LA DIFFERENCE

Peccaries have large heads and flat snouts like pigs. So how do you tell a peccary from a wild hog? Well, peccaries are typically smaller and have longer legs. They have straight tusks, while pigs have curved ones (though farmers typically remove their pigs' tusks). In addition, peccaries have three toes on their hind foot; pigs have four. Yet if you ever come face to face with one of these beasts, you probably won't want to examine teeth or count toes. What's the best way? If the beast is giving off a rank aroma, you've got a peccary on your hands (really, their smell is the stuff of legend). Good luck.

11. PECCARY (JAVELINA)

The collared peccary (Pecari tajacu) is named for a light band of hair around its neck. Looking at one of these animals you might think, "Hey! That's just a hairy pig." Not so fast. Though they're related to pigs (and to hippos, too), javelina are not quite pigs. They're like a New World version of pigs. They range from the American Southwest all the way down to northern Argentina. In the United States, they're only found in Arizona, New Mexico, and Texas. Javelinas live in small herds and eat a variety of plants, seeds, fruits, nuts, and small insects. They especially love prickly pear and agave. These animals have terrible eyesight, but have excellent smell, thanks to their pig-like noses. Smell is the main way they identify their fellow herd members, with whom they form strong bonds. Smell you later, pal.

CLASSIFICATION

KINGDOM: *Animalia*

PHYLUM: *Chordata*

CLASS: *Mammalia*

ORDER: *Artiodactyla*

SUBORDER: *Suina*

FAMILY: *Tayassuidae*
(New World pigs)

BY THE NUMBERS

10 YEARS	*Typical life span of a javelina in the wild, though some in captivity live beyond twenty years.*
2 FEET	*Normal height of a peccary.*
50	*Size of a large peccary herd. Small ones might have just six members.*

TEARJERKER

For a school science project, an eight-year-old Arizona boy set up a camera next to a dead peccary. On the video, other peccaries were seen visiting the body again and again, like a funeral procession. They sniffed and touched the deceased, and some even slept next to it and defended it from coyotes. Were they mourning a fallen friend? Scientists aren't sure, but it seems likely.

IT'S GOOD TO HAVE FRIENDS

A horse in the wild would never choose to live alone and has solid reasons for living in herds. While grazing, with its head buried in grass, a lone horse is vulnerable because it can't see approaching danger. In herds, horses share the burden of keeping lookout, which is a great stress reliever.

Clydesdale
Horse
(Male)

12. HORSE

The relationship between humans and horses goes back for thousands of years. Humans first domesticated horses around 6,000 years ago, and they've been among our staunchest friends and closest allies ever since. This animal (*Equus ferus caballus*), more than any other, has been at the center of human progress. They've carried us, worked for us, fought for us, and died for us. They've impacted our culture in countless ways—in stories, books, songs, movies, and even in language. You know many horsy sayings like, "Don't look a gift horse in the mouth," "horseplay," "hold your horses," and "get off your high horse," to name just a few. Even today, when horses are no longer necessary for pulling our carts or fighting with us in our battles, there remains a deep spiritual bond between people and their horses and that will never change.

WILD AND FREE

Many years ago, some horses were set free by their masters. Others escaped. The descendants of those feral horses are called mustangs, and they roam the open range in ten western states and are about as wild as a horse can be. The majestic mustang still symbolizes the spirit and freedom of the American West.

CLASSIFICATION

KINGDOM: *Animalia*

PHYLUM: *Chordata*

CLASS: *Mammalia*

ORDER: *Perissodactyla*

FAMILY: *Equidae*

GENUS: *Equus*

SPECIES: *E. ferus*

SUBSPECIES: *E. f. caballus* (*Domesticated horse*)

BY THE NUMBERS

60 MILLION	*Estimated number of horses worldwide.*
3 HOURS	*Average time horses sleep each day, mostly in naps while standing.*
10 GALLONS	*The amount of saliva a typical horse produces each day; an average human makes only 0.19 gallons.*

A DOGGED DEFENDER

Donkeys are very affectionate and form unusually strong bonds, especially with other donkeys. If a buddy is taken away, a donkey will get very depressed. Donkeys can even form bonds with animals of a completely different species. For this reason, they've been used as substitute guard dogs or to protect flocks of sheep or goats.

13. DONKEY

Donkeys (*Equus africanus asinus*) are the underappreciated cousins of horses. Also known as burros or jackasses, donkeys are descended from the wild ass of north Africa. Today, wild donkeys live in the American Southwest. Compared to horses, donkeys might have a reputation for being more stubborn, yet donkeys have nothing to be ashamed of. They're quite intelligent. That legendary stubbornness? It's really just the donkey being smart. A donkey considers any command carefully and refuses to do anything it thinks is dangerous. Donkeys are also a lot tougher than horses. They're sturdier, stronger pound-for-pound, require less food and water, and live longer. Horses are flight animals and will bolt if startled, whereas donkeys are not easily panicked. They'll stand their ground and fight.

CLASSIFICATION

KINGDOM: *Animalia*

PHYLUM: *Chordata*

CLASS: *Mammalia*

ORDER: *Perissodactyla*

FAMILY: *Equidae*

GENUS: *Equus*

SPECIES: *E. africanus*

SUBSPECIES: *E. a. asinus (Donkey)*

BY THE NUMBERS

UP TO **25** **YEARS**	*The amount of time a donkey can still remember people, places, and other donkeys.*
95%	*The percentage of its food a typical donkey can digest and use, meaning donkey manure is not a good fertilizer.*
50+ **YEARS**	*Typical lifespan of a donkey— they can live for a long time!*

HORSE OF A DIFFERENT COLOR

Donkeys can reproduce with horses. The offspring of a male donkey and a female horse is called a mule. Mules combine the size and speed of horses, with the gentle nature, long life, and hardiness of donkeys. It's a sweet combination. Sign me up.

Norway
Rat

LEAP TALL BUILDINGS IN A SINGLE BOUND?

In many ways, rats are like super rodents. They can spring over four-foot-wide chasms. They have razor sharp teeth and can chew through lead pipe, aluminum sheeting, electrical cable, and even cinderblock. Expert climbers, they can scale shear brick walls and scamper up trees. Rats can even tumble from a height of fifty feet without any harm. They can scurry along wires like it's nothing. Water? No problem. Rats are wonderful swimmers with amazing stamina. All this means there are very few buildings that can keep them out.

14. RATS AND MICE (INVASIVES)

The three most common rats and mice in North America are all invasives. They're descendants of critters that sailed from Europe as stowaways in the 1600s and 1700s. Here's the Terrible Trio: the Norway rat (*Rattus norvegicus*), often called the brown or common rat; the black rat (*Rattus rattus*); and the house mouse (*Mus musculus*). All three live in close association with humans. They destroy our crops and eat our food, fouling what they don't eat by peeing and pooping on it. They cause untold damage to property, seriously threaten our health, and sometimes even bite us in our sleep—often for no apparent reason. Rats carry parasites, like lice, mites, and fleas, and also many diseases, such as bubonic plague (the Black Death), spotted fever, and Rat Bite Fever. It's been said that more people have died because of rats than in all the wars combined. Rats!

CLASSIFICATION

KINGDOM: *Animalia*

PHYLUM: *Chordata*

CLASS: *Mammalia*

ORDER: *Rodentia*

FAMILY: *Muridae*

GENUS: *Rattus* (Rats) / *Mus* (Mic

BY THE NUMBERS

25,000	*Approximate number of poop pellets that a single rat can leave during jus one year.*
3 DAYS	*How long rats can swim or tread water.*
14,000	*Approximate number of people in the U.S. each year who report rat attacks.*

Black Rat

JUMPIN' JEHOSHAPHAT!

*The desert kangaroo rat (*Dipodomys deserti*) is only active at night when it's cool. Since it's dark and oh-so quiet in the desert at night, the rodent will often blunder upon a coiled rattlesnake. Yet when the snake strikes, it strikes out. Whiff! Nothing but empty air. That's because the rat has jumped clear and is sailing high overhead. All this happens super fast in the blink of an eye. Of course, the rattler does win occasionally and eats the rodent, but usually that doesn't happen. Ninjas generally win.*

Banner-
Tailed
Kangaroo
Rat

15. RATS AND MICE (NATIVES)

Plenty of rats and mice were already living in North America long before Europeans brought over their pesky Old-World cousins. These indigenous, or native, rodents include woodrats (packrats), kangaroo rats, pocket mice, deer mice, white-footed mice, wood mice, and muskrats. They can be just as interesting as bigger animals.

CLASSIFICATION

KINGDOM: *Animalia*

PHYLUM: *Chordata*

CLASS: *Mammalia*

ORDER: *Rodentia*
(Rats, mice, and all other rodents)

Grasshopper Mouse

KILLJOY

Unlike other rodents, the southern grasshopper mouse is a hardened predator. This bad boy lives in the deserts of the U.S. and Mexico, a dangerous neighborhood full of shady characters, many venomous. You think it's worried? No way. Yes, it often dines on easy victims like grasshoppers, beetles, and worms, but it also goes after tarantulas, snakes, and even other mice. But that's not all. It sometimes scarfs down venomous centipedes and even deadly scorpions. Sure, a scorpion will use its stinger on the mouse, but nothing happens. That's because the mouse's innards actually change that killer venom into a painkiller!

BY THE NUMBERS

90 TIMES	*How much bette the hearing of a kangaroo rat is than human hearing.*
70 MILLISECONDS	*Reaction time of a kangaroo rat. A human's average reaction time is about 250 milliseconds.*
70%	*The approximat percentage of times a kangaroo rat escapes from rattlesnakes.*

THAT MAGIC BEAVER BUTT

Beavers don't see too well, so they experience the world mainly through smell. A beaver's personal scent arsenal consists of a pair of castor sacs and a pair of anal glands. Both produce smelly liquids that are unique to each beaver. They're used to mark territory and to tell each other apart (we recognize faces; they recognize scents). The dark, syrupy liquid from the castor sacs is called castoreum and, surprise, it's not stinky but smells like vanilla! Even weirder, castoreum has been used in perfumes and even in foods to enhance vanilla flavoring. Just think about that the next time you order ice cream.

American Beaver

16. BEAVER

The beaver (*Castor canadensis*) is the famously busy semiaquatic rodent. It has webbed hind feet and a flat tail, which it employs like a rudder. Also, a beaver comes equipped with see-through, inner eyelids that act like swim goggles. Since it's rather clumsy on land, it needs deep water for protection. So, if a pond or lake isn't handy, it will make one by damming a river or stream with a dam made from logs, branches, or stones—whatever's handy. Beavers mate for life and form unusually strong family units. The beaver family home is the beaver lodge, a large, dome-shaped structure that's very sturdy—even a grizzly can't break in. It has two underwater entrances, like a front and back door. Inside, there's a raised platform, well off the water, that's covered with bark, grass, and wood shavings. It all makes for a comfy-cozy dwelling, especially during winter.

IRONCLAD TEETH

Each beaver has four large, very sharp front teeth: two up top, two on bottom. It uses these to clip saplings, to gnaw off bark, and even to cut down entire trees. Ever chipped a tooth? Well, beavers usually don't, even with all that heavy-duty chomping and gnawing. That's because beaver teeth have a protective coating that contains iron!

CLASSIFICATION

KINGDOM: *Animalia*

PHYLUM: *Chordata*

CLASS: *Mammalia*

ORDER: *Rodentia*

FAMILY: *Castoridae*

SUBFAMILY: *Castorinae*

GENUS: *Castor (Beavers)*

BY THE NUMBERS

15 MINUTES	*Maximum time that beavers can stay underwater without surfacing.*
110 YARDS	*The typical width of a beaver dam (about the length of a football field), with the largest being over a mile wide.*
ABOUT **1** INCH	*Length of the four beaver incisors (front teeth).*

EARTHMOVERS

Pocket gophers not only
use their front claws while
digging, but their four
large incisors, too. While
removing earth with these
teeth, a gopher can close
her lips beneath them.
This keeps dirt from
getting into her mouth.
Then, after loosening soil
with tooth and claw, she
kicks it behind her using
her hind feet. Next, she
somehow manages to
reverse direction by doing
a somersault inside her
cramped tunnel. Then all
she has to do is push the
dirt through the length
of her tunnel with chest
and paws, then out her
entrance hole. She looks
just like a little bulldozer.

Pocket
Gopher

17. POCKET GOPHER

Pocket gophers, usually called just gophers, are burrowing rodents. They spend most of their time underground and are rarely seen. However, their mounds are a different story. If a gopher's around, you'll see piles of dirt everywhere. Gophers can make several mounds each day, about seventy each month, and about two hundred each year. They're busy little critters! Gophers are plant eaters and get their meals in three ways. A gopher may eat roots that she stumbles upon while digging. Or she may go topside and feed on above-ground vegetation, never straying far from her hole. Or, she may pull entire plants from below into her tunnel. Now you see it—*bloop!*—now you don't. Though gophers cause lots of property damage, they actually benefit the environment by stirring up the soil. So don't get too upset with them when they start digging up your lawn.

CLASSIFICATION

KINGDOM: *Animalia*

PHYLUM: *Chordata*

CLASS: *Mammalia*

ORDER: *Rodentia*

SUPERFAMILY: *Geomyoidea*

FAMILY: *Geomyidae* *(Gophers)*

BY THE NUMBERS

UP TO **200** **YARDS**	*Length of all the tunnels in a gopher's burrow complex. That's as long as two football fields.*
1 **BODY LENGTH**	*How far a gopher is willing to stray from its hole while feeding aboveground.*
1 **TON**	*Estimated weight of soil that a gopher can move to the surface each year.*

DEEP POCKETS

Suppose a gopher's tummy is already full, yet she finds more delicious greenery that she wants to save for later. How does she carry it to her underground storeroom? She puts it in her pockets. A gopher has two pockets, each lined with fur. That's why she's called a "pocket" gopher. There's one on the outside of each cheek.

Gray
Squirrel

SQUIRREL QUALITY CONTROL

Eastern gray squirrels (Sciurus carolinensis) are nuts about nuts. However, not just any nut will do. Whenever a squirrel finds one, she must put it through a whole battery of quality-control tests. First, she'll give it the smell test to make sure it's not rotten or diseased in any way. Then, she'll spin the nut in her paws, checking for holes and cracks—a cracked nut would rot in the ground and must be rejected. And last but not least, there's the shake test. The squirrel will hold the nut in her jaws and quickly flick her head. This looks like a nervous tick but is actually her way of verifying there's a seed inside; the flick rattles the seed. After all, it's not the nut's hard, dry shell that she's interested in—it's the tasty seed inside with its delicious and nutritious protein and fat. If the nut passes all these tests, it makes the team. Hoarding is serious business!

18. SQUIRRELS AND CHIPMUNKS

These busy little rodents are usually divided into three types: tree squirrels, ground squirrels, and flying squirrels. Tree squirrels are the most well-known. They nest in trees, have long, bushy tails, and are active year round. That means they must store food for winter. Ground squirrels make their homes by digging burrows. Being hibernators, they sleep during winter so they won't need to store any food. Chipmunks are a type of ground squirrel, yet they only half hibernate, waking up every few days to eat. So, they have to store winter food just like non-hibernators. Chipmunks have cheek pouches on the inside of their mouths. They use these like shopping bags to carry nuts back to their burrows, up to seven at a time for each pouch!

BY THE NUMBERS

10,000	The number of nuts a gray squirrel can gather in one season.
25%	Estimated percentage of a squirrel's buried nuts that get stolen.
160	The number of acorns that a chipmunk can gather in one day.

A DEN OF THIEVES!

The forest is full of furry little thieves, and our squirrel knows it. After finding a nut, she must hide it. But suppose some sneaky villain is watching to see where she buries it? To foil onlookers, she'll use the old fake-burial trick (technically called "deceptive caching"). Oh sure, she'll go through the motions of burying her nut, making a great show of digging in the leaves and soil. Yet she's kept that nut tucked in her mouth the whole time. She might fake-bury several times before doing the real-bury.

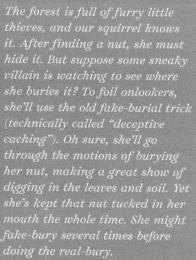

Northern Flying Squirrel

THE FUR WILL FLY

The *"wings"* of flying squirrels are made of skin. There's a furry fold of skin between each wrist and ankle and another between each ankle and the tail. When a squirrel stretches out his legs to fly, these skin folds stretch out too, converting his entire little body into a square parachute. Also, the hairs on his tail flatten, so it acts like a rather nice rudder. Flying squirrels need to get high to be able to glide. The higher they are, the farther and faster they can glide. That's why they only live in places with lots of tall trees. A squirrel gets airborne by using his great jumping ability to launch himself. Then he steers by moving his tail or his arms and legs.

19. FLYING SQUIRRELS

First, an important technicality: flying squirrels can't actually fly. Bats are the only mammals that can truly fly. Flying squirrels are gliders, like furry little paper airplanes. But they're much than that. They have exquisite control over their glides and are capable of making sharp turns, controlling their speed, adjusting their angle of descent, and even maneuvering around branches. They're omnivores, eating nuts, berries, lichen, mushrooms, insects, eggs, and even young birds. They nest in tree holes. Flying squirrels don't hibernate, though they're much less active during winter. When it's really cold, they congregate together in the same tree cavity to keep warm. Most squirrels are diurnal, or active during the day. Flying squirrels are nocturnal, which means they're active at night. To help them see in the dark, they have super big, bulging eyes. My what big eyes you have!

GLOW-IN-THE-DARK RODENTS

If you're out in the woods at night in an area where flying squirrels live, take a UV flashlight with you. If you shine that thing on a flying squirrel, the squirrel immediately glows a brilliant pink! Molecules in the squirrel absorb the invisible UV light and convert it into light that we can see (in this case, pink light). This is called fluorescence. Scientists still don't know why squirrels have this feature. It's another of nature's mysteries.

CLASSIFICATION

KINGDOM: *Animalia*

PHYLUM: *Chordata*

CLASS: *Mammalia*

ORDER: *Rodentia*

FAMILY: *Sciuridae*

SUBFAMILY: *Sciurinae*

TRIBE: *Pteromyini (Flying squirrels)*

BY THE NUMBERS

2	*The number of flying squirrel species in North America: the Southern flying squirrel and the Northern flying squirrel.*
150 FEET	*Distance that a flying squirrel can glide from a height of sixty feet.*
50	*The most flying squirrels that were found together in a tree cavity.*

DOWNTOWN

Prairie dogs live in complex underground burrows. Each entrance hole is surrounded by a mound of dirt. The mounds are one to three feet high and up to ten feet wide. They serve as lookout towers for spotting predators and as dams to prevent flood waters from pouring in. Each hole descends six to fifteen feet below the surface and opens onto tunnels that link the dwelling chambers of each family. The whole intricate web of tunnels and chambers is called a prairie dog town, and its residents are called a prairie dog colony.

Prairie
Dog

KISSING COUSINS

When two prairie dogs meet, they often stand on their hind legs, embrace, and give each other a big smooch! This affectionate greeting serves to strengthen bonds between members of the same coterie. But it's also a way to tell friend (a member of the same coterie) from foe. If a prairie dog doesn't kiss just right, he's a stranger and must be driven away.

20. PRAIRIE DOG

When early explorers came to America's prairie region, they saw many furry little creatures scampering over the landscape. They often made high-pitched, squeaky noises that the explorers thought sounded like barking (it actually sounds more like bird chirping). So they called them "little dogs" or "the wild dog of the prairies." Yet prairie "dogs" are not dogs at all, but burrowing rodents of the squirrel family. They can often be seen standing like lawn statues among a field of cone-shaped mounds. Prairie dogs are highly social creatures. Their basic social unit is the coterie, which is a family group consisting of one adult male and one to four adult females along with their juveniles and pups. Life is good in the prairie-dog coterie, where there's always someone to talk to.

FAST TALKERS

Prairie dogs talk to each other—a lot. One purpose of all the yipping and yapping is to help everyone work together to defend the colony. Prairie dogs have been observed making coordinated attacks to drive away predators, like rattlesnakes. They also cooperate in keeping lookout. Whenever a prairie dog on guard duty spots danger, he sounds the alarm by yipping. Then, other prairie dogs either join the warning chorus or run and hide in their burrows.

CLASSIFICATION

KINGDOM: *Animalia*

PHYLUM: *Chordata*

CLASS: *Mammalia*

ORDER: *Rodentia*

FAMILY: *Sciuridae*

TRIBE: *Marmotini*

GENUS: *Cynomys (Prairie dogs)*

BY THE NUMBERS

5	*The number of species of prairie dog. The black-tailed prairie dog (Cynomys ludovicianus) is the most common.*
1,000 ACRES	*Typical spread of a prairie dog town.*
25,000 SQUARE MILES	*Largest prairie dog town ever recorded—about the size of West Virginia!*

45

Groundhog

A SHADOWY PAST

Some people believe that Groundhog Day originated from an ancient Christian festival called Candlemas, held every February 2. Over time, a tradition developed that if the sun was shining on Candlemas, then the rest of the winter would be long and hard. If it was cloudy, then warm weather was just around the corner. Later, in Germany, an animal and its shadow were added to the superstition, only it was a hedgehog (or sometimes a badger). If the hedgehog saw its shadow, then a "Second Winter" was in the cards. Germans who colonized Pennsylvania brought this tradition with them. However, since no hedgehogs were available, they substituted the groundhog.

21. MARMOT AND GROUNDHOG

Marmots are large, burrowing ground squirrels. The most famous marmot is the groundhog (*Marmota monax*), the only animal with its own major holiday. It's also known as a "woodchuck." Marmots are very social creatures and live in small colonies. In contrast, groundhogs are anti-social and just want to be left alone. Whether groundhog or marmot, these little guys are true hibernators. That means they must pack away as much food as possible during summer so that they'll have enough fat reserves to survive the long winter. By fall, they can get pretty porky. When marmots hibernate, they go dormant and crank their body functions way down. Body temperatures drop from 99° F to 40° F and heart rates from one hundred beats per minute to only four.

BY THE NUMBERS

80%	*Percentage of a marmot's time spent underground.*
39%	*Success rate of groundhog weather forecasting—in other words, bet against the groundhog.*
16 TO 2	*Decrease in marmot breaths per minute during hibernation.*

AIN'T NO SUNSHINE WHEN SHE'S GONE

It probably won't surprise you to learn that there's nothing special about a groundhog's shadow. Yes, he does drag himself out of bed around Groundhog Day. But he doesn't wake to examine his weather charts or to check his barometer. All he's looking to do is scope out the local girls—really!

SPLITTING HARES?

Hares (also called jackrabbits) are a lot tougher than rabbits. They're bigger, have larger ears and longer legs, and can run much faster. Rabbits usually live in burrows (the well-known rabbit hole), while hares dwell in nests above ground. In addition, baby hares are ready to face the world almost from birth, with eyes wide open, fully haired, and ready to run after only an hour. On the other hand, baby rabbits are born helpless, eyes closed, no hair, and are dependent on their mother for a longer time.

Common Hare

DUNG DINERS CLUB

Rabbits enjoy nothing better than a nice meal of poop. A bunny does this because there's still food value in his feces after just one pass through his body. So, wanting to get his money's worth, he gobbles up the soft and sticky first-pass poop. After that, the poop comes out as dried, little pellets because every last nutritional goody has been squeezed out of it. Now the bunny has no reason to eat these pellets and won't. Eating second-pass poop—now that would be gross!

22. RABBIT AND HARE

Rabbits, unfortunately, seem like they were born to be eaten. These unlucky creatures are hunted by just about every predator under the sun. They have few defenses other than great eyesight, a keen sense of smell, good hearing (those famous ears), and strong hind legs that allow them to sprint up to twenty miles per hour. But this often isn't enough. Sadly, most bunnies don't even survive their first year in the wild. Fortunately, they're very good at making replacements. Whenever a female rabbit mates, it's like instant babies—just one month is all it takes and Mom's up to her rabbit-ears in little bunnies. Plus, she can mate again almost immediately. This allows her to fit in three litters each year, while the babies can join in the baby-making fun after only a few months. Breed like a rabbit indeed!

Cottontail Rabbit

CLASSIFICATION

KINGDOM: *Animalia*

PHYLUM: *Chordata*

CLASS: *Mammalia*

ORDER: *Lagomorpha*

FAMILY: *Leporidae (Rabbits and hares)*

BY THE NUMBERS

270 DEGREES	*How far around a rabbit's ears can rotate, which helps him hear approaching predators.*
3 FUNCTIONS	*Number of functions for rabbit ears: excellent hearing, air conditioning, and "talking" with other rabbits.*
37 BODY-LENGTHS PER SECOND	*Speed of a hare. The cheetah can only do twenty body-lengths per second.*

"PANZER PIGS"

Since armadillos have long, piggish snouts and often make pig-like grunts, they're sometimes called "armored pigs." During World War II, captured German prisoners held at P.O.W. camps in Texas referred to the strange beasts as panzerschwein. *In German, that means—you guessed it—"armored pig."*

Nine-Banded Armadillo

23. ARMADILLO

The nine-banded armadillo (*Dasypus novemcinctus*) is a fantastically odd-looking creature, like a weird hybrid between a rat, a rabbit, and a snail. It's the only mammal that carries its own suit of armor. Armadillos have poor eyesight but excellent hearing. They also have pretty good sniffers. They're expert diggers, with powerful legs and impressive claws, which they use to dig burrows and to unearth their favorite insect snacks. After exposing some tasty underground morsels, like a colony of ants, an armadillo will lap 'em up with a long tongue covered in sticky saliva. Armadillos don't hibernate, and because they have low metabolisms and hardly any fat or fur, they don't do well in cold—that shell is useless against it. That's why they prefer warm regions, like the southeastern United States. Armadillos are rather tasty when eaten; some people say the meat tastes like chicken, others like pork. They've been called Texas turkeys, Hoover hogs, and poor man's pork. However, care must be taken, since some armadillos carry the leprosy bacterium. I think I'll have a cheeseburger instead.

CLASSIFICATION

KINGDOM: *Animalia*

PHYLUM: *Chordata*

CLASS: *Mammalia*

SUPERORDER: *Xenarthra*

ORDER: *Cingulata* (*Armadillos*)

BY THE NUMBERS

20%	*Approximate number of armadillos in the southeaster United States that carry the leprosy bacterium.*
4 BABIES	*Number of babies in a typical litter. Nine-banded armadillos almost always have identical quadruplets.*
5 FEET	*How high an armadillo can jump when startled.*

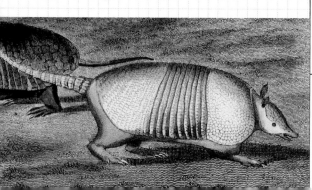

MOLE SUPERSTAR

The star-nosed mole gets its name from the twenty-two tentacles surrounding its nostrils like a starburst. The entire nose is only about the size of your fingertip, but it's stuffed with 100,000 nerve endings; your entire hand has only 17,000. The touch information it gathers is used to create an image inside the mole's brain, just like our brains create an image from light, or bat brains create one from sound. So this mole actually "sees" with that bizarre star—it's like nose, eyes, and hands all rolled into one.

Star-Nosed
Mole

24. **MOLE**

A "fossorial" animal lives underground and digs for a living. That's the mole. Moles are small creatures, about four to nine inches long, with cylindrically-shaped bodies that easily slip through tunnels. They have short, muscular legs and over-sized paws bristling with claws. This makes them excellent diggers. A mole is nearly blind. Its eyes are tiny and usually covered with fur. Its ears aren't too great either. They don't even have outside ear flaps like we have. That's okay, because more than sight or hearing, a mole relies on its amazing nose. That nose not only smells extremely well, it's hyper-sensitive to touch; there are thousands of touch receptors stuffed into that little thing!

CLASSIFICATION

KINGDOM: *Animalia*

PHYLUM: *Chordata*

CLASS: *Mammalia*

SUPERORDER: *Laurasiatheria*

ORDER: *Eulipotyphla*

SUPERFAMILY: *Talpoidea*

FAMILY: *Talpidae*

SUBFAMILY: *Scalopinae*
(*New World moles*)

BY THE NUMBERS

40	Approximate number of species of mole worldwide.
99%	The percentage of time Eastern moles (*Scalopus aquaticus*) spend underground.
250 MILLISECONDS	The time it takes a star-nosed mole to identify something as prey and eat it. It's the world's fastest eater.

Hairy-Tailed Mole

BURN, BABY, BURN

The air we breathe is a mixture of oxygen and nitrogen gas, but it's the oxygen that our bodies crave. That's what we need to convert food into energy. What's leftover is carbon dioxide (CO_2) gas, and that's what we breath out. If we're ever trapped inside a sealed space and the level of oxygen gets too low or the carbon dioxide too high, we're in trouble! But moles don't have this problem. They can breathe the same air for a long time, because they have special blood that's able to handle oxygen-depleted, CO_2-enriched, air.

THIS MEADOW AIN'T BIG ENOUGH FOR THE BOTH OF US

Shrews are not particularly fond of each other. If two of them meet while out hunting, you can bet there's gonna be a brawl. There are no rules in these ultra-lightweight bouts, much less referees. Clawing is legal, biting even better. Since the action is so violent, both contestants will use up tons of energy, and if they don't get another meal quick, it's curtains. Probably for this reason, the loser usually gets eaten.

North
American
Least
Shrew

25. SHREW

Shrews are close cousins of moles. They are quite small, only two to five inches from tip to tip (nose to tail). At first glance, a shrew might look like a mouse, but mice have much bigger eyes and ears, plus longer tails. Shrews are predators and pretty good ones, too. They have to be, since they must consume food at a mind-boggling rate. If a shrew goes even a few hours without eating, it might die. That's because they have super souped-up metabolisms. Their little motors run fast and burn hot. A shrew's teensy heart can beat up to 1,300 times every minute when stressed, which is all the time. Not surprisingly, shrews don't live very long. Most don't even make it past their first year. This little animal truly lives fast and dies young.

CLASSIFICATION

KINGDOM: *Animalia*

PHYLUM: *Chordata*

CLASS: *Mammalia*

ORDER: *Eulipotyphla*

FAMILY: *Soricidae* (Shrews)

BY THE NUMBERS

200	The number of mice a short-tailed shrew can kill with its venom.
5 FEET	Length that a water shrew (Sorex palustri can scamper over the surface of water.
12	Number of movements a shrew can make every second. Stop drinking that coffee, pal!

A BITE WORSE THAN ITS BARK

The short-tailed shrew (Blarina brevicauda) produces a potent venom that kills or paralyzes prey, similar to snakes. And now things take a truly ghastly turn, because shrews usually don't kill their prey before eating it. They like their food fresh, as in still-living fresh! They will often cache (store and hide) a victim after immobilizing it, saving the poor devil for a rainy day. Since it's still alive, the meal definitely stays fresh. Brrrr!

Marsh Shrew

Pipistrelle

SOUND INSIGHT

Bats aren't blind—they can see with their eyes.
Yet in the dark, eyes aren't much use. Also, a
bat needs to navigate in three dimensions, not
just two—a much tougher task. To keep track of
where she is, a bat requires a more sophisticated
system of navigation than sight: echolocation.
To echolocate is to locate using sound echoes.
While flying at night, she will emit many high-
frequency cries that are ultrasonic (beyond sound
or people's ability to hear). When these cries
reflect off objects and return to her sensitive
ears, she's able to construct a 3D image in her
head. Echolocation gives the position, size, and
distance of insects the bat might want for dinner.
Repeating the cries tells their speed and direction
of flight. So, blind as a bat? Not even close.

26. BATS

Most people don't like bats. Traditionally, we've associated them with darkness, death, and evil. Yet bats are actually harmless, even remarkable creatures. They're the only mammals that can fly. And they're quite good at it, too, thanks to those creepy yet amazing wings. A bat's wings are actually its hands, with finger bones that spread over the entire surface. This hand-wing design gives the bat exquisite control over the movement and shape of its wings, much better than birds have. This allows bats to fly with incredible agility and maneuverability. The flying tricks they can do are jaw-dropping. In a flat-out sprint between a bird and a bat, a bird might win, but a bat could fly circles around any bird. They hunt using a technique called echolocation (see opposite page).

THE REAL BATMAN

Can people echolocate, like bats? As it turns out, we can. Most of us don't, of course, because we don't need to. But Dan Kish, who went blind as a baby, has taught himself how to echolocate using clicking sounds. Now he can ride a bike, hike on unfamiliar trails, and navigate through strange cities. Echolocation is just a form of sonar, which stands for Sound Navigation And Ranging. So Dan calls his technique "flashsonar." And most surprising of all, when he echolocates, he uses the same area of his brain that people use for seeing. So he's actually constructing a visual image in his head, like bats do. Amazing!

CLASSIFICATION

KINGDOM: *Animalia*

PHYLUM: *Chordata*

CLASS: *Mammalia*

CLADE: *Scrotifera*

ORDER: *Chiroptera (Bats)*

BY THE NUMBERS

500	*Number of plant species that depend heavily on bats for pollination, including agave and bananas.*
20 MILLION	*The number of bats in the Bracken Bat Cave in Texas, the world's largest bat colony.*
$30 BILLION	*Value of the pest-control service provided by bats.*

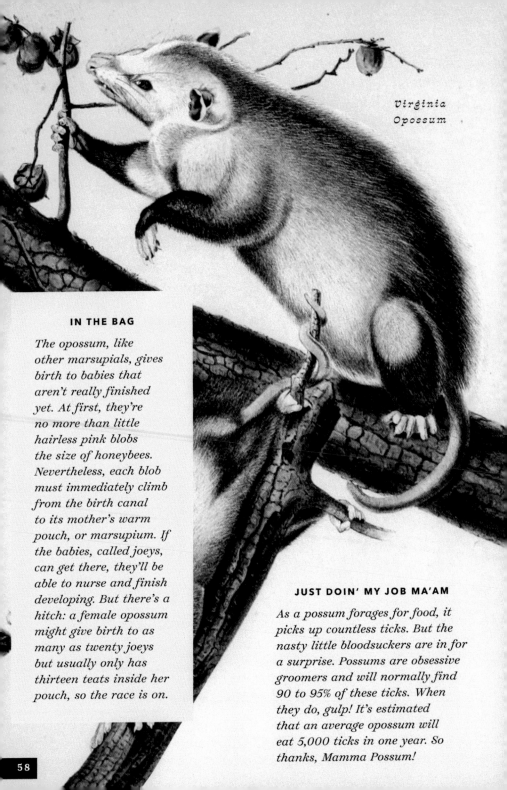

Virginia
Opossum

IN THE BAG

The opossum, like
other marsupials, gives
birth to babies that
aren't really finished
yet. At first, they're
no more than little
hairless pink blobs
the size of honeybees.
Nevertheless, each blob
must immediately climb
from the birth canal
to its mother's warm
pouch, or marsupium. If
the babies, called joeys,
can get there, they'll be
able to nurse and finish
developing. But there's a
hitch: a female opossum
might give birth to as
many as twenty joeys
but usually only has
thirteen teats inside her
pouch, so the race is on.

JUST DOIN' MY JOB MA'AM

As a possum forages for food, it
picks up countless ticks. But the
nasty little bloodsuckers are in for
a surprise. Possums are obsessive
groomers and will normally find
90 to 95% of these ticks. When
they do, gulp! It's estimated
that an average opossum will
eat 5,000 ticks in one year. So
thanks, Mamma Possum!

27. OPOSSUM

The Virginia opossum (*Didelphis virginiana*), or "possum" for short, is North America's only marsupial, which is an animal that carries its young in a pouch like a kangaroo. An opossum's paws are more like very nimble hands, each with five delicate, well-separated fingers. The big toe on each hind paw is actually an opposable thumb like on your hand. This helps possums grab branches. Also, a possum has a prehensile tail, a tail that can grab onto things. It's used like a fifth hand. If really frightened, a possum will faint and "play dead"—lolling tongue, foamy drool, the works—from which we get the saying, "playing possum." However, the possum is not playing. It's actually in a catatonic state, like a deep sleep. The idea here is that predators often don't like to eat pre-dead things. The possum even releases a foul-smelling, green liquid from its anal glands so it smells dead. Possum for dinner? Ah, no thanks.

CLASSIFICATION

KINGDOM: *Animalia*

PHYLUM: *Chordata*

CLASS: *Mammalia*

INFRACLASS: *Marsupialia*

SUPERORDER: *Ameridelphia*

ORDER: *Didelphimorphia*

FAMILY: *Didelphidae (Opossums)*

BY THE NUMBERS

1/2 INCH	*Length of a newborn opossum joey.*
4 HOURS	*The maximum time a possum might be unconscious while "playing possum."*
1/200 OF AN OUNCE	*Weight of a newborn joey. That's about 1/10 the weight of a paperclip.*

BACK PACK

At about two months, the baby joeys are big enough to go outside the pouch. Now they all pile onto their mother's back and ride around with her on her nightly rounds. Since the expression "piggyback ride" has nothing to do with pigs, perhaps it should be changed to "possum-back ride."

Long-Tailed
Weasel

PUT ON YOUR DANCING SHOES

Sometimes a short-tailed weasel, while chasing a difficult-to-catch animal like a large rabbit, will suddenly stop and launch into a bizarre, psycho dance! Sometimes called the "weasel war dance," the performance pace is fast and furious. Leaping and twisting, turning and spinning, even rolling on the ground are all part of the act. It looks like the little guy has lost his marbles. The dumbfounded bunny can only stare in wonder and disbelief. Yet as the innocent rabbit watches the show, the little weasel is slowly inching closer. By the time the bunny realizes what's happening, it's too late. Rabbit for lunch.

28. WEASEL

Weasels are the lead members of the *Mustelidae* family, also called the weasel family. We have three species in North America: the least weasel (*Mustela nivalis*), the long-tailed weasel (*Mustela frenata*) and the short-tailed weasel (*Mustela erminea*, also called the ermine or stoat). They all have long tubular bodies, arched backs, short legs, stretched-out necks, and long tails. As carnivores (meat eaters), they come fully equipped with strong claws and an impressive arsenal of sharp teeth. They're also incredibly flexible. It's like they have rubber for bones or are filled with water! This body plan allows them to snake through some very tight places—like rodent burrows. Weasels are one of the few animals that play as adults. If they are well fed, they'll run, bounce, prance, and ricochet around in their quest for fun. They're be the life of any party!

LEAST BUT NOT LAST

The least weasel is the smallest carnivore on earth, measuring only six to nine inches from tip to tip. But don't be fooled. His powerful jaws and sharp teeth easily puncture a rodent's skull. He then hauls the corpse back to his burrow, where at first he only eats the brains!

Least Weasel

CLASSIFICATION

KINGDOM: *Animalia*

PHYLUM: *Chordata*

CLASS: *Mammalia*

ORDER: *Carnivora*

FAMILY: *Mustelidae*

SUBFAMILY: *Mustelinae*

GENUS: *Mustela (Weasels)*

BY THE NUMBERS

UP TO **50**	*Number of corpses found inside a least weasel's den—chamber of horrors indeed!*
2 **OUNCES**	*Average weight of a least weasel—the same as just twelve sheets of paper.*
164	*A least weasel's bite force quotient (bite force divided by body size); the African lion's is only 112 and the gray wolf's 136.*

American
Fisher

29. MARTEN AND AMERICAN FISHER

The American marten (*Martes americana*) and the American fisher (*Pekania pennanti*) are two more tough mustelid predators with typical long, slender bodies. Both are creatures of the forest. Martens are about the same size as mink and prey on squirrels, mice, voles, and hares. They have a distinctive orange throat patch that biologists can use like a fingerprint to tell one marten from another. Fishers are bigger animals, though slightly smaller than wolverines. Despite their name, they don't fish. They eat many of the same things as martens—and also porcupine, which is no small feat. Both martens and fishers have curved, semi-retractable claws, so they easily climb trees. They also have hind paws that rotate backward so they can climb down tree trunks head first. Unfortunately, both animals are still trapped today for their fur.

CLASSIFICATION

KINGDOM: *Animalia*

PHYLUM: *Chordata*

CLASS: *Mammalia*

ORDER: *Carnivora*

FAMILY: *Mustelidae*

SUBFAMILY: *Guloninae*
(*Martens, fisher, tayra, and wolverine*)

BY THE NUMBERS

30-60 MINUTES	*Approximate length of fisher porcupine battles.*
60 MILES	*How far a fisher might travel during a three-day period searching for food.*
3 MONTHS	*Time it takes a baby marten to reach full size. They grow very fast.*

American Marten

DINNER TABLE TUMMY

Sea otters have breakfast in bed every day, plus lunch and dinner too. Flat on their backs, they use their tummy like a meal tray. They'll often place a rock there to help break open shell-food. Just a quick bash or two is all it takes to get at the tasty morsels inside. After eating, clean-up is a snap. They just roll over a few times in the water and presto, everything is cleared away. They're masters of the quick spin-clean.

GATOR GOBBLER

Despite their cuteness, all otters are voracious predators. For example, one river otter was actually recorded attacking a five-foot long alligator. It ambushed the gator from behind, biting its neck, then held on while the gator thrashed about and exhausted itself. Cute but deadly!

North American River Otter

30. OTTER

There are two types: sea otters (*Enhydra lutris*) and river otters (*Enhydra lutris*). What's the difference? Sea otters are much larger than their river cousins, weighing about four times as much, and are nearly fully aquatic. River otters are only semiaquatic, meaning they split time between land and water. They also have longer and rounder tails and are well-known for their playfulness. Sea otters don't need to drink as much water as land animals, so they can get most of what they need from food. Remarkably, they can also drink salty sea water. They're one of the few mammals that can accomplish this difficult trick. Sea otters are considered a keystone species, meaning they are vital to the survival of a whole ecosystem—in their case, the kelp forest ecosystem along the Pacific coast.

CLASSIFICATION

KINGDOM: *Animalia*

PHYLUM: *Chordata*

CLASS: *Mammalia*

ORDER: *Carnivora*

FAMILY: *Mustelidae*

SUBFAMILY: *Lutrinae* (Otters)

BY THE NUMBERS

ALMOST **1** **MILLION**	*The number of hairs per square inch in sea otter fur. Otters were relentlessly hunted for this luxurious fur.*
300+ **FEET**	*Maximum depth to which sea otters can dive underwater.*
7 **MILES PER HOUR**	*Top speed of a river otter in water (Olympic swimmers can go only about 4.5 miles per hour).*

Sea Otter

WATER BEDS

In contrast to river otters, sea otters are very clumsy on land. They're in water almost all the time and can usually be found floating on their backs, eating, grooming, or sleeping. They often form all-boy or all-girl groups called rafts. Some otters even hold hands (paws) during their naps to keep from drifting away as they dream their otter dreams. Other otters wrap themselves in kelp before taking a snooze for the same reason.

WHAT IT MEANS TO BE BADGERED

Badgers have terribly nasty dispositions and, when riled, are ferocious and tenacious fighters. Few animals will mess with a badger—not more than once, anyway. With massive claws and canines, a badger is well-equipped to dish out punishment. Most animals get the message. Even more impressive, badgers can take it just as much as they can dish it out. Due to their thick, loose skin and low profile, would-be predators just can't get a good grip on them. Also, badgers can release a strong, musk-like scent, which many animals find unpleasant (though not as bad as a skunk's). One way or another, it's usually the big-bully predator that retreats!

American
Badger

31. BADGER

The American badger (*Taxidea taxus*) is another relative of weasels and otters. Badgers are short, stocky animals, built wide and low to the ground. They're true digging machines. From the claws of steel on each foot, to the powerful, stubby legs, to that drill-shaped head, everything about a badger is sturdy, heavy-duty, and says, "digger." Yes, the dirt really flies when a badger is digging! Badgers are also master underground builders. Their burrows can be quite impressive, with multiple chambers and often lined with grass—very cozy indeed.

CLASSIFICATION

KINGDOM: *Animalia*

PHYLUM: *Chordata*

CLASS: *Mammalia*

ORDER: *Carnivora*

FAMILY: *Mustelidae*

SUBFAMILY: *Taxidiinae*

GENUS: *Taxidea*

SPECIES: *T. taxus* (*American badger*)

BY THE NUMBERS

3 FEET-PER-MINUTE	*A typical badger's estimated rate of digging, depending on soil.*
29 HOURS	*Length of a badger's nap during winter (they don't truly hibernate).*
1.75 INCHES	*Length of claws on a badger's front paws. That's crazy long!*

BLIND MAN'S BLUFF

It's generally believed that a badger's eyesight is its weakest sense. No matter. Not only can they smell and hear very well, they're also capable of feeling underground movements with their super-sensitive claws and forepaws. So, when a badger is out looking for lunch, he might dig briefly, feel in the dirt with his paws, then shift position and dig and feel again. Repeating the process, he finally locates an underground victim. Then, he explodes into a fit of wild digging and presto, there's a rodent in his jaws.

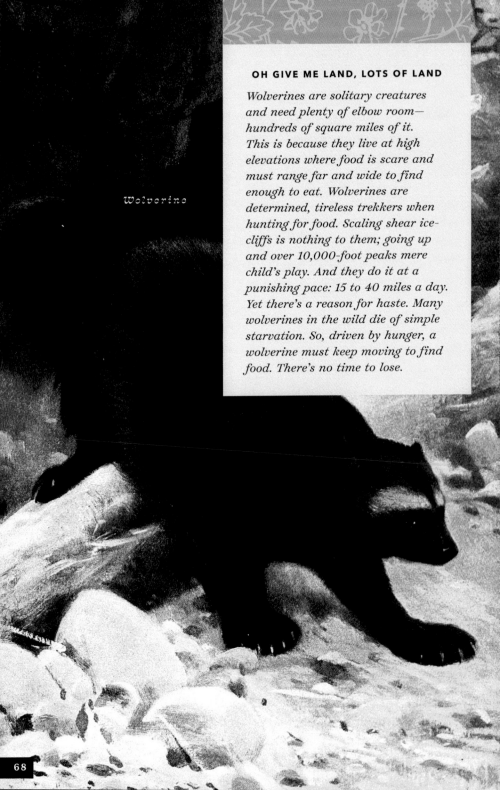

Wolverine

OH GIVE ME LAND, LOTS OF LAND

Wolverines are solitary creatures and need plenty of elbow room— hundreds of square miles of it. This is because they live at high elevations where food is scare and must range far and wide to find enough to eat. Wolverines are determined, tireless trekkers when hunting for food. Scaling shear ice-cliffs is nothing to them; going up and over 10,000-foot peaks mere child's play. And they do it at a punishing pace: 15 to 40 miles a day. Yet there's a reason for haste. Many wolverines in the wild die of simple starvation. So, driven by hunger, a wolverine must keep moving to find food. There's no time to lose.

32. WOLVERINE

Fearless, tough, tenacious—that's the wolverine (*Gulo gulo*). It's the largest member of the weasel family, though still not a big animal—only as big as a medium-sized dog. Yet the wolverine has a reputation for strength and viciousness out of all proportion to its size. They can drag a moose or caribou carcass for miles, bend steel traps into pretzels, and gnaw through wooden walls and ceilings. In the past, they would drive trappers crazy, stealing animals from their traps, raiding and trashing their cabins, or pilfering their food. The wolverine looks like a small bear and has light markings rather like a skunk, hence one of its nicknames: "skunk bear." It has a stout, well-muscled body, short legs, semi-retractable claws, and a powerful bite capable of crunching frozen meat and bone. Among all the tough customers in the weasel family, wolverines are the toughest of the tough.

CLASSIFICATION

KINGDOM: *Animalia*

PHYLUM: *Chordata*

CLASS: *Mammalia*

ORDER: *Carnivora*

FAMILY: *Mustelidae*

GENUS: *Gulo*

SPECIES: *G. gulo*
(*Wolverine*)

BY THE NUMBERS

9 MILES	*The estimated distance a wolverine can gallop without rest.*
30 MILES PER HOUR	*Top speed of a wolverine.*
2 TIMES	*The amount a wolverine's paw expands when pressed to the ground—instant snow-shoe!*

DON'T SAY I DIDN'T WARN YOU

Skunks are inoffensive creatures; they just want to be left alone and aren't looking to spray anyone. So they'll usually give plenty of warning before giving you a blast, like arching their backs, stomping their feet, or hissing. A skunk can't afford to waste ammo, since he only carries enough for three or four shots. Once the chamber is empty, it can take up to ten days for a reload. That's ten days of being defenseless, so spraying is only a last resort!

Striped
Skunk

33. SKUNK

Skunks are justifiably famous for their foul-smelling musk, which is truly horrible. According Charles Darwin, it's a "fetid oil, which brings on violent sickness and running at the nose. Whatever is once polluted by it, is forever useless." Though it's a skunk's only defense, it sure is a good one. Being sprayed by a skunk is so unpleasant that few predators will ever mess with one. (One of the few that will is the great-horned owl, but that doesn't count because the bird can't even smell.) It's a good thing, too. Skunks are slow, awkward, poor climbers, and nearly blind. It's not unusual for a skunk to tumble into a pool, into a window well, or to blunder into someone's house through a doggie door. Once inside, good luck trying to get him out. He's probably going to make a big stink about it.

Hooded Skunk

DEADEYE

If a skunk does decide to give you a blast, he'll squeeze his anal glands. This causes a vile, yellowish oil to shoot out through two butt nipples. He can adjust the spray from a fine mist to a thin, laser-like stream, which can be aimed with pin-point accuracy. How good? Good enough to nail you square in the eyes and blind you from a distance of over ten feet!

CLASSIFICATION

KINGDOM: *Animalia*

PHYLUM: *Chordata*

CLASS: *Mammalia*

ORDER: *Carnivora*

SUPERFAMILY: *Musteloidea*

FAMILY: *Mephitidae*
(Skunks and stink badgers)

BY THE NUMBERS

1 IN 1,000	*Fraction of people who can smell the skunk stink, the lucky devils.*
5	*Number of skunk species in the U.S. The striped skunk (*Mephitis mephitis*) is the most common.*
2-20 MILES	*How far away people can smell skunk spray, depending on weather conditions.*

Common
Raccoon

FORTUNE FAVORS THE BOLD

Boldness and curiosity make for great learners. As a result, bold, curious animals like raccoons tend to learn very quickly—and cities offer raccoons a rich variety of learning situations. So it's no surprise that urban raccoons are actually smarter than their country cousins— and probably getting smarter all the time.

34. RACCOON

Raccoons are extremely intelligent and adaptable creatures. They're nocturnal and have excellent night vision. Also, they're good swimmers, amazing climbers, and can digest just about anything. Yet a coon's most valuable assets are a pair of remarkably nimble hands (forepaws) and a hyper-developed sense of touch. Raccoons understand their surroundings by constantly touching, handling, and fiddling with everything—"seeing" with their hands. They often dunk things in water, not to wash them, but because wetting seems to make their paws even more sensitive. Like people, raccoons are omnivores and opportunistic; they'll eat whatever they happen to find. In the wild, they hunt rodents, frogs, eggs, and crayfish, among other things. Yet around people, the menu changes to include chickens, crops, garden items, and especially leftovers from trash cans.

CLASSIFICATION

KINGDOM: *Animalia*

PHYLUM: *Chordata*

CLASS: *Mammalia*

ORDER: *Carnivora*

FAMILY: *Procyonidae*

GENUS: *Procyon*

SPECIES: *P. lotor*
(Common raccoon)

BY THE NUMBERS

UP TO **35** **FEET**	*The approxima*[*distance a raccoon can fal*] *without injury—tough critters!*
2-3 **YEARS**	*Lifespan of a typical raccoon in the wild, though in captivity they can live up to twenty years.*
UP TO **3** **YEARS**	*Time span a raccoon can remember how to do some task (which, in the wild, is basically its entire lifetime).*

IT'S ALL RELATIVE

Yes, raccoons have very clever hands, but that's only compared to other animals. Their hands are nothing compared to your hands. For example, a raccoon could never use a pair of scissors. Human hands are one of our superpowers!

Though very rare, mountain lions do attack people. So, if you ever meet a mountain lion in the wild, whatever you do, don't run! Like all cats, cougars have a powerful instinct to pursue fleeing prey. By running, all you're doing is hanging a big sign around your neck saying: "Dinner is served. Come and get it!" Just remember this: who is prey and who is predator often depends not on who is stronger, but on who acts stronger. It's a question of bluffing, and cougars are suckers for a good bluff. So make yourself appear as big as possible. Spread your legs, open your jacket, and wave your arms. Also, speak loudly and firmly. Act like a predator and make that big cat think it's prey. As amazing as it might seem, it usually works.

DON'T ENTER THIS CAT IN A MARATHON

The Achilles' heel of cougars is their poor stamina. Sure, they're stupendously fast, but they tire quickly. The reason for this is that they have small hearts and lungs for such large, muscular animals. That's why cougars are ambush hunters. It takes less energy.

Mountain Lion

35. MOUNTAIN LION

The big wildcat of North America (*Puma concolor*) is commonly known by a confusing jumble of names, including mountain lion, cougar, puma, panther, and catamount. Whatever you call it, you'll probably never see one in the wild (and if you do, you're either very lucky—or very unlucky). Cougars are shy and elusive creatures. They're remarkably adaptable and can be found in a variety of ecosystems. They're also crazy athletic. For example, a mountain lion can run like the wind and leap up to eighteen vertical feet from a standing start. This makes them great ambush hunters. They usually hunt from dusk to dawn, waiting patiently to pounce on prey from behind and then deliver a lethal bite to the neck. This might seem cruel, yet nature is actually healthier when these big cats are on the prowl and doing their part to keep everything in balance.

CLASSIFICATION

KINGDOM: *Animalia*

PHYLUM: *Chordata*

CLASS: *Mammalia*

ORDER: *Carnivora*

SUBORDER: *Feliformia*

FAMILY: *Felidae*

SUBFAMILY: *Felinae*

GENUS: *Puma*

SPECIES: *P. concolor* (Mountain lion)

BY THE NUMBERS

16 MONTHS	*Age of cougar cubs when their eyes change from blue to gold.*
45 FEET	*Distance mountain lions can leap horizontally with a running start. Wow!*
50 MILES PER HOUR	*Top speed of a cougar. Remember: that's way faster than you.*

DON'T PET EVEN IF PURRING

Unlike other big cats, mountain lions can't roar, but they do make that typical, ripping wildcat screech. They can also growl, hiss, spit, and even meow and purr like house cats, the largest cats that can do so. Nice kitty, kitty.

SUPER HUNTER

Bobcats are excellent hunters and hunt prey with unrivaled patience and skill. These cats use all three hunting senses— sight, sound, and smell—to find prey, but rely mostly on sight. They have excellent vision, especially in dim light, where they see six times better than humans. Their eyes are also hyper- sensitive to movement. Once prey is spotted, they will creep up carefully and quietly, then make a quick ambush. Bobcats are superb athletes—quick, agile, coordinated, and powerful— with retractable claws, long, sharp fangs, and a powerful bite. Being such supercharged physical specimens, they can take down animals ten times their size, like deer.

Bobcat

36. BOBCAT

Of the three species of wildcat in the U.S. and Canada, the bobcat (*Lynx rufus*) is the most common. Yet even with all the bobcats out there, you'll probably never see one. With very few exceptions, if a bobcat doesn't want to be seen, you won't see it—and it never wants to be seen. They're much smaller than mountain lions, though about twice the size of ordinary house cats. A bobcat even looks like a house cat, with a distinctive facial ruff below each cheek and a spiky tuft at the tip of each ear. Its legs are unusually long in relation to body size, and the paws uncommonly large. Yet the weird thing about a bobcat compared to other cats is its short, "bobbed" tail. It's really stubby! Small body, long legs, stubby tail—a bobcat might look odd, but don't be fooled. Everything works purrrrfectly (yes, bobcats can purr too).

THE PREDATOR IN THE MIRROR

Go to the zoo and look at animal eyes. You'll notice that animals fall into two main categories: those with side-facing eyes and those with front-facing ones. In general, prey animals, like rabbits, have side-facing eyes to give them a wide field of vision. In contrast, predators, like bobcats, usually have front-facing eyes. This limits the field of vision but, in exchange, gives binocular vision, a sort of 3D image. This provides depth perception. Now look in the mirror. In which direction do your eyes face?

CLASSIFICATION

KINGDOM: *Animalia*

PHYLUM: *Chordata*

CLASS: *Mammalia*

ORDER: *Carnivora*

SUBORDER: *Feliformia*

FAMILY: *Felidae*

SUBFAMILY: *Felinae*

GENUS: *Lynx*

SPECIES: *L. rufus*
(Bobcat)

BY THE NUMBERS

30 MILES PER HOUR	*Maxiumum speed of a bobcat. Though something like a house cat, a bobcat is much faster and can go from zero to thirty in the blink of an eye.*
1 MILLION	*Estimated total number of bobcats in the world.*
5 INCHES	*Average length of a bobcat tail. It's a "bobbed" tail, after all.*

CRY FOUL

If you're ever camping in the great north woods and hear a scream in the night that seems to come straight from the infernal regions, don't worry. Roll over in your sleeping bag and go back to sleep. All's well. It's probably just a couple of lynx having a disagreement. When two males dispute—over territory, perhaps, or a female— instead of fighting, they engage in a good old-fashioned shouting match. And for such silent creatures, they can really raise an unholy racket when they want to. How they determine the winner is not known!

Canadian Lynx

37. CANADIAN LYNX

The Canadian lynx (*Lynx canadensis*) is a cold-weather specialist. Long legs and huge furry paws help the cat to hunt in deep snow. The paws even become bigger when walking because the toes spread—great snow shoes! The lynx is similar to its more common cousin the bobcat. It's not always easy to tell them apart—they even have the same stubby tail. Like bobcats and cougars, lynx are excellent hunters and superior athletes: fast, coordinated, and crazy leapers. Being mostly nocturnal, solitary, and secretive, lynx are rarely seen, just like it's two big-cat cousins. However, lynx are much pickier about where they live, preferring isolated, sub-alpine forests away from humans. They're also finicky about what they eat. Yes, they'll dine on mice, squirrels, birds, and even deer, but what they really crave is snowshoe hare. So if there's lots of hares around, there's gonna be lots of lynx. Hares and lynx are, well, linked.

CLASSIFICATION

KINGDOM: *Animalia*

PHYLUM: *Chordata*

CLASS: *Mammalia*

ORDER: *Carnivora*

SUBORDER: *Feliformia*

FAMILY: *Felidae*

SUBFAMILY: *Felinae*

GENUS: *Lynx*

SPECIES: *L. canadensis* (*Canadian lynx*)

BY THE NUMBERS

250 FEET — *Distance from which a lynx ca[n] spot a mouse.*

90% — *Percentage of the lynx's diet that consists of snowshoe hare.*

10 YEARS — *Length of a snowshoe hare population cycl[e] (the time it takes to go from many hares, to just a few, and back to many again). Lynx populations mirror this boom-bust cycle[.]*

HIT THE ROAD, JACK

Lynx have a serious streak of wanderlust. They sometimes make epic journeys, even farther than those of wolverines. Scientists suspect that the purpose of these trips has something to do with the snowshoe hare, though they really don't know at this point. Perhaps the cats just like to travel.

ALPHA-BETA SOUP

Wolves are very social creatures and live in packs. A pack is essentially a family unit, with a mother and father, sisters and brothers, and perhaps a few strays. The wolf pack is run according to a strict hierarchy (a top-to-bottom organization) in which each member is ranked. The top dogs, the alpha male and alpha female, are the father and mother. Other members in the pack are also ranked, all the way down to the omega wolf. The omega is often bullied and treated like a scapegoat or court jester. This seems mean to us, but the omega is vital to the pack. For example, it relieves tensions—having a punching bag helps wolves work out their anger issues. It's easier for everyone to get along with the omega on the job. When the omega dies, there is great mourning in the pack. They all get depressed, moping around with tails and heads drooping. Killers, yes, but they're really just a bunch of softies.

Gray
Wolf

38. WOLF

Perhaps no animal is more associated with the "dark side" of nature than the big, bad wolf. People have feared and hated this animal for centuries and hunted it relentlessly. The gray wolf (*Canis lupus*) is the largest member of the dog family. Gray wolves can be thirty-six inches high at the shoulder, four to six feet in length, and can weigh between 60 and 170 pounds. Wolves live and hunt in well-organized packs. The wolf pack is a chillingly efficient killing machine, capable of taking down much larger animals in smart, well-coordinated attacks. But there's another side to the wolf. The line between love and hate is often very thin. It's probably no coincidence that the world's most loved animal, the domesticated dog (*Canis lupus familiaris*), is just a reformed version of its most hated one, the gray wolf.

CLASSIFICATION

KINGDOM: *Animalia*

PHYLUM: *Chordata*

CLASS: *Mammalia*

ORDER: *Carnivora*

FAMILY: *Canidae*

GENUS: *Canis*

SPECIES: *C. lupus* (*Wolf*)

BY THE NUMBERS

1	*What makes a "lone wolf." Sometimes a wolf will leave the pack, usually hoping to find a mate.*
20 POUNDS	*Amount of food a single wolf can consume in a one sitting, hence, "wolfing it down."*
4X5 INCHES	*Typical size of a wolf paw, which is about the same as an adult human hand.*

THE LOOK OF LOVE

Though dogs and wolves are alike in many ways, there are also big differences. One of these is in their ability to bond with humans. Dogs express affection by looking at you. But in the wolf world, maintaining eye contact is viewed as a threat, a challenge, or an attempt to dominate. That's why wolves rarely look directly at each other. It's the same reason people don't make eye contact on a New York City subway. On a New York subway, people turn into wolves.

Coyote

A TRICKY BUSINESS

The coyote is prominent in many Native American stories. He always appears as a classic trickster character (a trickster is a creature who doesn't obey the rules and uses tricks or practical jokes to get what he wants or to escape danger). Here's an example of coyote cunning and trickery. Western ranchers have tried using guard dogs to prevent coyotes from preying on their sheep. For a time it seemed to work. But then the coyotes came up with a tricky countermeasure. One coyote would lure away the dogs, and the rest would swoop in on the sheep. Chalk up another one to the tricky trickster.

39. COYOTE

The coyote (*Canis latrans*) is a species of wild dog. Unlike their wolf cousins, which are found worldwide, coyotes are unique to North America—they're our wild dog. This is a beautiful animal, but also a highly intelligent one—tricky, cunning, crafty, clever, wily, devious, and sneaky are just *some* of the words that apply. Coyotes have proven again and again that they're masters of adaptation. They originally lived in the central plains and southwest deserts of the U.S. where they were known as prairie wolves. Thanks to their adaptability, they have expanded their range and are now found in nearly every corner of North America.

CLASSIFICATION

KINGDOM: *Animalia*

PHYLUM: *Chordata*

CLASS: *Mammalia*

ORDER: *Carnivora*

FAMILY: *Canidae*

GENUS: *Canis*

SPECIES: *C. latrans* (Coyote)

BY THE NUMBERS

19	Maximum number of pups in a coyote litter, though usually it's five to seven
IT TAKES 2	Like wolves, coyotes mate for life.
1919	The approximate year when the first coyote-wolf hybrid, the coywolf, was noticed in Ontario (eastern wolves were so few in number that they began mating with coyotes).

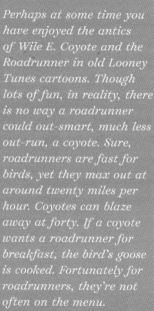

NO CRAZY CLOWN

Perhaps at some time you have enjoyed the antics of Wile E. Coyote and the Roadrunner in old Looney Tunes cartoons. Though lots of fun, in reality, there is no way a roadrunner could out-smart, much less out-run, a coyote. Sure, roadrunners are fast for birds, yet they max out at around twenty miles per hour. Coyotes can blaze away at forty. If a coyote wants a roadrunner for breakfast, the bird's goose is cooked. Fortunately for roadrunners, they're not often on the menu.

Red Fox

LEFTOVERS

A red fox is a master hunter and will keep hunting even when her tummy is full. So what does she do with all that extra food? In the wild, your next meal is never certain, so the fox will bury her leftovers in a top-secret hiding place called a cache (rhymes with stash). Foxes usually have several caches and will often go to great lengths to keep them secret from other animals. One fox was even seen backing away from a cache-stash, carefully erasing her paw prints. Now that's one foxy fox! Usually, foxes store food for only a day or two, but sometimes will let it age up to two months. The fox finds the cache again by relying mostly on memory. Then, it's rotten food for dinner!

40. FOX

When most people think "fox," it's usually the red fox (*Vulpes vulpes*) they have in mind, an animal with loads of star power—looks, brains, personality, dude's got it all. Red foxes are the largest and most common of the foxes, but are often confused with their cousin, the gray fox (*Urocyon cinereoargenteus*). Like the coyote, the red fox is very adaptable and can live in many habitats. They're perfectly happy dwelling near humans and can survive in farmland and even in cities. Unlike other canids, red foxes don't hunt in pairs or packs. They're loners. The exception to their loner ways comes when it's time to raise a family. Female foxes (called vixens) generally give birth in underground dens to four babies (called kits). Both the mother and father share the duty of providing for their family, but raising the rambunctious kits is left mostly to the mother.

DON'T BRING LABELS AROUND HERE

Biologists say the fox is a canid or canine—a member of the dog family. Yet many people, when looking at a fox, see its vertically-slit pupils, triangular ears, long tail, and slender build, and think, "Cat!" So, dog or cat? It's best to say, "neither." Like you, a fox is its own creature. A fox is a fox.

CLASSIFICATION

KINGDOM: *Animalia*

PHYLUM: *Chordata*

CLASS: *Mammalia*

ORDER: *Carnivora*

FAMILY: *Canidae*

GENUS: *Vulpes*
(*True foxes*)

BY THE NUMBERS

5 — *Number of species of fox in North America, the others being the Kit Fox (Vulpes Macrotis), the Swift Fox (Vulpes velox) and the Arctic Fox (Vulpes lagopus).*

1/3 — *Amount of a fox's total length made up by its tail. Big and bushy, the tail aids in balance and keeps the fox warm when curled round its body.*

Polar
Bear

THE NOSE KNOWS

A polar bear, like all bears, has a superior sense of smell, possibly the best in the animal kingdom. They can smell a whale carcass from over twenty miles away and even detect a seal under three feet of ice. Why are polar bears such super sniffers? First, they have very long noses, so the nasal mucosa—the part that does the actual smelling—is very large. And the olfactory bulb, the area of the brain dedicated to processing smells, is five times larger in bears than in humans. It's believed that polar bears can even smell seven times better than a bloodhound! Thankfully, there are no skunks in the artic.

41. POLAR BEAR

The polar bear (*Ursus maritimus*) is the top predator and marquee species of the Arctic. It's the largest bear on Earth, weighing 900-1600 pounds and measuring eight to ten feet from nose to tail. Polar bears need sea ice to survive, because that's where they mate and hunt for food. Out on the ice, a bear might crouch next to a seal hole for hours or even days waiting patiently for a seal to come up for air. A polar bear has special fur designed for maximum warmth. It's oily, which keeps water out, and hollow, which traps heat in. The hairs are translucent, which means they allow light to pass through to the bear's skin. Now here's a surprise. Under that snow-white fur, the bear's skin is actually all black, which is the best color at absorbing heat. Finally, beneath the skin is a thick layer of blubber that prevents heat loss. Polar bears have no problem staying warm. Their challenge is staying cool, especially as earth's climate continues to warm.

CLASSIFICATION

KINGDOM: *Animalia*

PHYLUM: *Chordata*

CLASS: *Mammalia*

ORDER: *Carnivora*

FAMILY: *Ursidae*

GENUS: *Ursus*

SPECIES: *U. maritimus*
(Polar bear)

BY THE NUMBERS

UP TO **12** INCHES	*Width of a polar bear's paws.*
25 MILES PER HOUR	*Sprinting speed of a polar bear on land. Don't let their size and lumbering walk fool you!*
4 INCHES	*Thickness of the blubber layer under a polar bear's skin.*

MASTERS OF WATER, SNOW, AND ICE

Polar bears are exceptionally strong swimmers and use their big front paws, which are slightly webbed, like paddles. They are fast in water and can go for many miles, hundreds if necessary. On snow, each foot pad is covered with small, soft bumps called papillae, which provide excellent traction.

FAT AND PEE FOR DINNER, AGAIN?!

Both black and brown bears go into a deep sleep during winter. Most people call this hibernation, though scientists point out that bears aren't true hibernators. In any case, during hibernation, a bear's metabolism is slashed by 75%. Its breathing and heart rate also go way down. Fortunately, since it doesn't eat or drink anything, it won't need to wake up to visit the bathroom. All nutrients necessary for survival come from "eating" its own body fat and recycling its urine (pee). Since bears "eat" themselves during winter, when they wake in spring, they'll be 15-40% lighter. What a great dieting idea!

42. BLACK BEAR

Besides the polar bear, there are two other bear species in North America: the black bear (*Ursus americanus*) and the brown bear (*Ursus arctos*). Black bears are the most common bears worldwide, so if you see a bear, chances are it's a black bear. They are opportunistic omnivores and will eat anything that's at hand (or paw), like berries, fish, insects, larvae, roots, grass, and other plants. They sometimes prey on big-hoofed animals like deer and elk, but usually only on the young or sick. They go for the easy pickings. Bears enjoy raiding beehives too, not only for the honey, which they love, but also for the honeycomb and larvae. Not only that, they will go for pet food, produce from gardens and fruit trees, and even garbage.

CLASSIFICATION

KINGDOM: *Animalia*

PHYLUM: *Chordata*

CLASS: *Mammalia*

ORDER: *Carnivora*

FAMILY: *Ursidae*

GENUS: *Ursus*

SPECIES: *U. americanus* (*American black bear*)

BY THE NUMBERS

100 TO 1	*Black bears outnumber brown bears by 100 to 1 in the U.S.*
10 DEGREES FAHRENHEIT	*Average drop in body temperature of a black bear during hibernation.*
2	*Number of times that a typical black bear breathes each minute while hibernating. And he snores, too!*

POWER NAP

A bear typically hibernates for four to seven months. If you or I were to stay in bed that long, our muscles would atrophy (get really small) and our bones would become brittle. None of this happens to a bear. It's able to get what it needs to maintain bones and muscles in tip-top condition from recycling its urine. Broken bones will even mend. That's one slick potty trick!

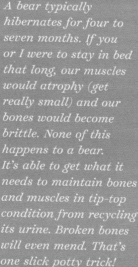

Once grizzlies were very common. Way back in the early 1800s, members of the Lewis and Clark Corps of Discovery (1803-1806) had many battles with these bears. Grizzlies attacked their canoes, ambushed hunting parties, and chased people up trees or into rivers. Clark wrote that they became "so troublesome to us that I do not think it prudent to send one man alone on an errand of any kind." The men were astonished by how tough the animals were. One bear was shot ten times, receiving five balls through the lungs, and was still able to swim across a river. Another was shot through the lungs, but still managed to chase the shooter half a mile.

Grizzly Bear

43. BROWN BEAR

The brown bear (*Ursus arctos*) is called the "grizzly" in much of North America because of its white-tipped hair. It's a beautiful animal: large, powerful, majestic, and defiant. This bear is a much more aggressive and ferocious animal than the black bear. That's why the grizzly subspecies is called *Ursus arctos horribilis*, the "horrible northern bear." Yikes! Actually, despite their reputation as blood-thirsty man-eaters, grizzlies typically eat mostly nuts, roots, tubers, grasses, berries, plus insects like ants, moths, and bees. Grizzlies also love fish, especially salmon, and occasionally prey on larger animals like elk, deer, and moose. Just like black bears, they'll take any people-food they can get their paws on. Don't give it to them!

SERIOUSLY, DON'T FEED THE BEARS

Feeding grizzly bears is an absolute no-no. Grizzlies seem to forage (look for food) using what's known as an optimal foraging strategy. They prefer grub with the most energy content (calories) for the least effort—the most bang for the buck. And human food gives plenty of bang. It's loaded with calories, especially compared to natural food sources. So once bears learn about people food, they'll keep coming back for seconds and thirds. Don't feed the bears.

KINGDOM: *Animalia*

PHYLUM: *Chordata*

CLASS: *Mammalia*

ORDER: *Carnivora*

FAMILY: *Ursidae*

GENUS: *Ursus*

SPECIES: *U. arctos*
(*Brown bear*)

BY THE NUMBERS

21 TIMES	*The average grizzly-human encounter is about twenty-one times more likely to cause serious injury than a black-bear-human encounter.*
30-40 MILES PER HOUR	*Top speed of a grizzly. Despite their size, they're incredibly fast. So, you're probably too close.*
4+ INCHES	*Length of a grizzly bear's claws.*

Californian
Sea Lion

44. SEA LION

Sea lions belong to a group of large aquatic mammals known as pinnipeds, which means "fin foot." Actually, sea lions don't have fins, they have flippers (*fish* have fins). At any rate, sea lions can be found along shorelines throughout the Pacific rim. A sea lion is rather awkward on land, but in water it's a thing of beauty. It can glide quickly and gracefully through its liquid element, turn on a dime, and even explode from the water in great leaps called "dolphining." When not in water, sea lions are commonly seen dozing lazily in the sun at haul-out sites. They are quite sociable creatures and will talk to each other for hours using loud barks, grunts, and other noises. Even when they have plenty of room to spread out, they'll cram close together or even pile on top of each other. Pinniped togetherness is a beautiful thing. There are six living species of sea lion, and of these, the ambassador species is the California sea lion (*Zalophus californianus*).

CLASSIFICATION

KINGDOM: *Animalia*

PHYLUM: *Chordata*

CLASS: *Mammalia*

ORDER: *Carnivora*

CLADE: *Pinnipedia*

FAMILY: *Otariidae*

SUBFAMILY: *Otariinae*
(*Sea lions*)

BY THE NUMBERS

1,000 FEET	*Depth to which California sea lions can dive.*
6,000 MILES	*Distance a Northern fur seal can travel each year while at sea in search of food.*
100	*Number of small rocks in an average California sea lion's stomach. No one knows what they're for*

SURF'S UP DUDE

California sea lions are curious, playful creatures, particularly the young. They can often be seen frolicking together, sometimes playing games like underwater tag. They might even make a toy from some unfortunate sea creature like a starfish.

Ringed Seal

Harp Seal

A SEAL NEEDS EARS LIKE A HOLE IN THE HEAD

Want to know how to tell a "fake" seal from a "true" seal? "Fake" seals have ears and belong to the eared-seal family Otariidae. *Sea lions and fur seals are Otariids. "True" seals don't have ears. They belong to the earless-seal family* Phocidae. *The most common Phocids are harbor seals (*Phoca vitulina*). Phocids do have holes in their heads where the ears should be, plus all the proper ear-gear inside; they just don't have those outside thingies we call ears. Since they have the inner ear equipment, seals can hear just fine, both in and out of water. Who ever heard of such a thing?*

45. SEAL

You've probably noticed that seals and sea lions look alike. Naturally, they're often confused. For example, the trained "seals" that perform at zoos, aquariums, and circuses are actually sea lions. Seals couldn't even begin to do the tricks and acrobatic stunts that sea lions are capable of. This is because sea lions have strong, well-developed fore-flippers and can rotate down their hind ones into a walking position. In contrast, a seal's fore flippers are stubby little things, while the hind ones are basically useless on land. Out of water, the only way seals can move is to wiggle and jiggle their bodies, allowing them to scoot like bloated worms. Yet once in water, they're transformed. Now movement is almost effortless. Seals are the quiet pinnipeds. They don't make that awful racket that their sea-lion cousins do. They're strong, silent types.

CLASSIFICATION

KINGDOM: *Animalia*

PHYLUM: *Chordata*

CLASS: *Mammalia*

ORDER: *Carnivora*

CLADE: *Pinnipedia*

FAMILY: *Phocidae (Earless seals), Otariidae (Eared seals)*

BY THE NUMBERS

40%	*Harbor seal milk is forty percent fat—yummy.*
100 TO 10 **BEATS PER MINUTE**	*When diving, a harbor seal reduces its heartrate from about one hundred beats per minute to about ten to conserve oxygen*
30 **MINUTES**	*Length of time a harbor seal can remain underwater, though dives usually last about three minutes.*

Common Seal

GOOD VIBRATIONS

Lots of mammals have whiskers, known technically as vibrissae. These are special hairs that connect to super-sensitive nerves. The vibrissae function as another sensory organ, like ears and eyes. Seals and sea lions have super deluxe vibrissae. They're so sensitive and well-developed that they can detect the slightest underwater vibration.

READY FOR THE DEEP END

When it comes to deep-water diving, elephant seals are the pinniped champions of the world. They routinely dive to depths of 2,000 feet but can descend to over 5,000 feet. Also, though they usually stay down for twenty to twenty-five minutes, they can last for up to two hours. But here's the really crazy part. Back on the surface, they'll only need two to three minutes to catch their breath. Then it's back to the inky darkness below. They do this over and over for weeks at a time, morning and night. Scientists still don't know exactly how they do it.

46. ELEPHANT SEAL

The Northern elephant seal (*Mirounga angustirostris*) is the largest pinniped in the Northern hemisphere. These enormous animals come ashore twice each year at a few favorite spots in California and Baja California, once to breed and once to molt (shed fur). The rest of the year, they're out in the open ocean, feeding on deep-sea creatures. Mature males have big droopy noses like elephants. They're also huge, XXXXXL huge, weighing up to 5,000 pounds—that's 2 ½ tons! Females don't have droopy noses and are much smaller, only about one third as big as the bulls. Elephant seals might look big and blubbery and lazy, but they desperately need all that insulation. Deep in the ocean depths, the water is icy, usually just above freezing. Being warm-blooded creatures, these seals would freeze without blubber to stay warm. So don't think badly about those jiggling rolls of fat!

IN THE ARENA

Elephant seals have their own version of the rut where bulls battle for females. Unlike deer and elk, these guys often draw blood. They're like blubbery gladiators. And success in the arena is all about size—biggest bull wins. So, when out at sea foraging, a bull must gain as much weight as possible.

CLASSIFICATION

KINGDOM: *Animalia*

PHYLUM: *Chordata*

CLASS: *Mammalia*

ORDER: *Carnivora*

CLADE: *Pinnipedia*

FAMILY: *Phocidae*

TRIBE: *Miroungini*

GENUS: *Mirounga (Elephant seals)*

BY THE NUMBERS

5,690 FEET	*Maximum recorded dive of an elephant seal—that's ove one mile deep.*
13,000 MILES	*Distance an elephant seal can travel on it foraging trips sea.*
10 POUNDS	*The average daily weight gain of elephan seal pups while nursing.*

THE "LITTLE" (1,200-POUND) MERMAID

Did the legends of mermaids all start with misunderstood manatees? Apparently. Scientists now believe that all the tales of sailors seeing mermaids were really just sightings of manatees or their cousins, dugongs. Christopher Columbus himself mistook some manatees for mermaids during his first voyage to the New World. According to his journal, he "quite distinctly saw three mermaids, which rose well out of the sea." But he was rather shocked by their appearance. "They are not so beautiful as they are said to be." No kidding, Chris.

West Indian
Manatee

47. MANATEE

Most marine mammals, even whales, eat other animals. Manatees are different—they eat plants. They sleep ten to twelve hours a day and spend most of their remaining time eating. Manatees live in coastal waters, estuaries, and rivers, peacefully grazing on sea grass and other aquatic plants. That's why they're often called "sea cows." Even though they look fat with their roly-poly bodies, manatees actually don't have much fat. With low metabolisms and without fat to keep them warm, manatees can't tolerate cold water for long—around 68° F seems to be as low as they can go. If the water gets any colder, the manatees must go to where the water is heated, like at natural hot springs. Most manatee deaths are caused by humans, but fortunately, people are now trying to prevent this. Let's hope they succeed.

LIP SERVICE

Despite their nickname, manatees aren't related to cows. In fact, their nearest relatives on land are elephants! And just like an elephant's trunk, a manatee's droopy upper lip can grab onto things. It can even move its left lip separately from the right lip, just like two little lip-hands. Not only that, the whiskers on a manatee's lip are amazingly agile, like tiny fingers, which also helps when grabbing things.

CLASSIFICATION

KINGDOM: *Animalia*

PHYLUM: *Chordata*

CLASS: *Mammalia*

ORDER: *Sirenia*

FAMILY: *Trichechidae*

SUBFAMILY: *Trichechinae*

GENUS: *Trichechus (Manatees)*

BY THE NUMBERS

40-60 YEARS	*Lifespan of a manatee.*
100-150 POUNDS	*Amount of food a manatee can eat in just one day. That's a lot of salad!*
20 MINUTES	*Length of time resting manatee can hold their breath. When swimming, it's only three to five minutes.*

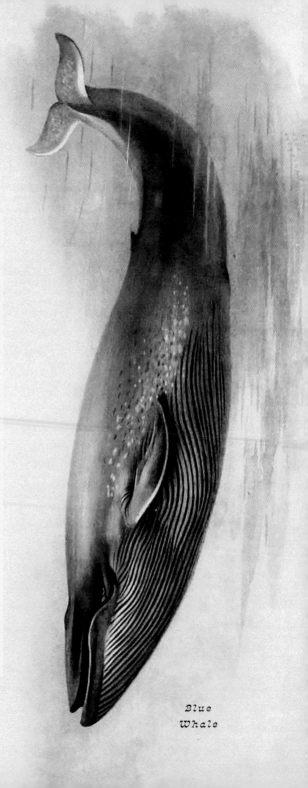

WHALE OF A SCALE

Whales are not only the biggest animals on earth today—they're the biggest ever. And the all-time champ is the blue whale. But wait a minute, you say. Weren't dinosaurs really big, too? Well, yes and no. Yes, some were longer and taller, but that's because they had tails and necks that were super long and skinny. That's cheating. What really matters is weight, and in a weight comparison, the blue whale crushes any dinosaur, even the mega Titanosaur. You could plop two Titanosaurs on a scale, and they still wouldn't weigh as much as a single blue whale. Of course, your scale would have to be as big as a house—a really big house.

Blue
Whale

48. BLUE WHALE

Whales come in many shapes and sizes, but there are basically two types: toothed whales and baleen whales. Baleen whales are the big ones, the "great whales." And the greatest of them all is Old Big Blue. The blue whale (*Balaenoptera musculus*) feeds almost exclusively on krill. These are shrimp-like zooplankton. Blues spend their summers in icy polar waters gorging on krill, then migrate thousands of miles to warm waters for winter. Unfortunately, the magnificent blue whale is an endangered species. If you're ever out whale watching and happen to see Big Blue, you're one lucky mammal.

CLASSIFICATION

KINGDOM: *Animalia*

PHYLUM: *Chordata*

CLASS: *Mammalia*

ORDER: *Artiodactyla*

INFRAORDER: *Cetacea*

FAMILY: *Balaenopteridae*

GENUS: *Balaenoptera*

SPECIES: *B. musculus*

BY THE NUMBERS

10,000 GALLONS	Volume of wate that a blue whale can engu with its big, big mouth.
200 TONS	Weight of a large blue whale, which is 400,000 pounds, or about 5,000 eleven-year-old kids!
3 TONS	The weight of a blue whale calf after birth, making it already one of the largest animals on earth.

BIG MOUTH

A blue whale can scarf down up to 8,000 pounds of krill each day. That's around three million of the little beasties. How does it manage to catch so many? Like all whales in the family Balaenopteridae, the blue whale has an expandable mouth. Pleated grooves running from chin to belly can stretch out like an accordion, forming a large feeding sac.

GONE FISHING

Some humpbacks use a remarkable hunting technique called bubble-net fishing. First, a group of humpbacks finds a school of small fish. Then, one of them circles below the fish, blowing air out her blowhole that surrounds them in a shimmering curtain of bubbles. Fish don't like air, so this traps them in a fizzy fish corral. The other whales act as herders, preventing escapes and driving the fish to the surface. On a signal, all the whales attack. They break the surface together, mouths wide open and surrounded by a sea of bubbling foam and flapping fish. Feeding frenzy!

MAKE YOUR OWN KIND OF MUSIC

All baleen whales grunt and groan, but some species actually sing. And the undisputed whale Meistersinger is the humpback whale. But don't go expecting a humpback to sing any of your favorite songs. Groans, moans, cries, chirps, and whistles are the best he can do. When he puts these all together, the "songs" are eerie, other-worldly, and beautiful, all at the same time. Scientists still haven't figured out why they sing.

Humpback Whale

49. HUMPBACK WHALE

The humpback whale (*Megaptera novaeangliae*) is one of nature's great performers. Breaching, fluking and flippering are just some of the acts on the program. Breaching is when a whale shoots out of the water and slams down with a crash and a splash. It's guaranteed to bring down the house. Fluking and flippering are more crashing and splashing, only using the tail flippers, called flukes, or a fore flipper. Being mammals, all whales have lungs and must breathe air. So they come equipped with blowholes atop their heads. After surfacing, a humpback exhales air from her blowhole. When the water vapor in her warm breath hits the cold, outside air, it forms droplets of water which we can see. This is her whale spout. It's just like seeing your breath on a cold, wintry day. Thar she blows, matey!

A WHALE OF A TALE

When feeding, a humpback will occasionally "swallow" a diver on accident. Yet have no fear. Though the diver fits easily into her cavernous mouth, she can't actually swallow him because her throat's too small. So she spits him out. Blech! I almost swallowed a human!

CLASSIFICATION

KINGDOM: *Animalia*

PHYLUM: *Chordata*

CLASS: *Mammalia*

ORDER: *Artiodactyla*

INFRAORDER: *Cetacea*

FAMILY: *Balaenopteridae*

GENUS: *Megaptera*

SPECIES: *M. novaeangliae (Humpback whale)*

BY THE NUMBERS

10 FEET	*Height of a typical humpback wha spout.*
2	*Number of blowholes. (Humpbacks, like all baleen whales, have a double blowhol and in the shap of a heart. Hou cute!)*
15 INCHES	*Width to which a humpback's throat can stretch.*

SMILE WHEN YOU SAY THAT

We've all seen that warm "dolphin smile." As humans, we can't help thinking, "Oh, what friendly, happy creatures!" That's what smiles mean to us, right? Yet a dolphin's "smile" is hardwired—that's just the way his jaw is shaped. He couldn't frown even if he wanted to. So don't be fooled; dolphins aren't people. They're extremely smart and versatile predators. A dolphin will keep that warm, friendly smile even as it's eating you. That's the dolphin way.

Bottlenose
Dolphin

50. DOLPHIN

The dolphin is a type of toothed whale. All whales are smart, but dolphins are on another level entirely. They're quick learners, wicked-good problem solvers, and have excellent memories. They also show a wide range of emotions and are skilled communicators. Good thing, too, since dolphins are quite the social animals. They form strong bonds with each other and interact in complex ways. They're also chatterboxes. The amazing variety of sounds they make includes whistles, squeaks, clicks, groans, and others we can't even describe. We still don't know what it all means. Some scientists believe dolphins actually have a language. People have even spent years trying to decipher it. Whether we'll ever be able to speak Dolphinish is still uncertain. One thing's for sure: trained dolphins can understand our language way better than we understand theirs.

CLASSIFICATION

KINGDOM: *Animalia*

PHYLUM: *Chordata*

CLASS: *Mammalia*

ORDER: *Artiodactyla*

INFRAORDER: *Cetacea*

SUPERFAMILY: *Delphinoidea*

FAMILY: *Delphinidae (Oceanic dolphins)*

BY THE NUMBERS

36 — *Number of dolphin species worldwide. Two of the more common types are the short-beaked common dolphi* (Delphinus delphis) *and the bottlenose dolphin* (Tursiops truncatus).

10 FEET — *Height a spinne dolphin can lea out of the wate usually while doing lots of spins and turn*

BRAINIACS

Dolphins have really big brains. In fact, they have the biggest brains in relation to body size of any animal, except for humans. Their brains are also very wrinkled (unlike face wrinkles, brain wrinkles are good since intelligence is linked to how wrinkly a brain is).

**BUSHEL
& PECK
BOOKS**

ABOUT THE PUBLISHER

Bushel & Peck Books is a children's publishing house with a special mission. Through our Book-for-Book Promise™, we donate one book to kids in need for every book we sell. Our beautiful books are given to kids through schools, libraries, local neighborhoods, shelters, nonprofits, and also to many selfless organizations who are working hard to make a difference. So thank you for purchasing this book! Because of you, another book will find itself in the hands of a child who needs it most.

Printed in the United States
by Baker & Taylor Publisher Services